Endorsements

Colleen Lanigan's book effectively provides spiritual healing to those who struggle with guilt or sadness from a suicidal incident of a beloved. Sometimes the death of a loved one is an awakening message to the survivors. Colleen's book is a must read!

—MARGUERITE DOYLE,
  PRESIDENT, PACE TANZANIA, LTD

Colleen's aim is always to enlighten both herself and others with God's manifested truth—to learn and grow, and then share in faith. She has an unquenchable desire to discover and apply His wonders that many of us can learn from.

Light shines brightest when the darkness is darkest. Colleen's journey and epiphanies will undoubtedly touch and bless many who are looking for a trusted source of light in their lives or circumstances.

—KAREN HAYES
  BOARD MEMBER, ILLINOIS FAMILY INSTITUTE;
  FORMER ILLINOIS STATE DIRECTOR,
  CONCERNED WOMEN FOR AMERICA

i

Through scientific research and narrative accounts, Colleen Lanigan demonstrates how our minds, just like our bodies can heal from trauma that shatters our lives. This book offers an intriguing, hope-filled message that healing is available to our brain and nervous system—a fact not often understood in conventional medicine.

—MONA HENNEIN
PRESIDENT AND CEO,
FOUNDER, LIFE FOCUS COMMUNICATIONS

There is a light within each of us and when we meet someone who is like minded, the connection is immediate. This is what happened when I met Colleen Lanigan in Oberammergau, Germany. For us, it was the glow of the Holy Spirit. I've always known the importance of the mind, body and spirit and Colleen shares this so beautifully in her book.

—CHAPLAIN SUSAN STAFFORD, PH.D.

THE NERVOUS SYSTEM: A SYSTEM OF LIGHT

Colleen Lanigan

The Nervous System: A System of Light

Cover image: "Brain neurons synapse functions illustration" by vampy1 (123RF) © 123RF.com Image ID: 23541412

LIBRARY OF CONGRESS CATALOGING-IN-PUBLICATION DATA

Lanigan, Colleen

The Nervous System: A System of Light

ISBN: 978-0-692-79047-2

1. Neuroscience 2. Neurophysiology and neuropsychology 3. Holistic medicine

Printed by CreateSpace, An Amazon.com Company

To learn more on this subject or contact the author:

www.neurohealthsystems.com

lanigan.colleen@yahoo.com

To my tender,
        loving God

And to those
        who affected me so

Contents

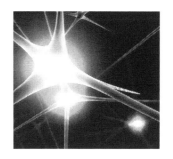

Introduction

Uniqueness of the Nervous System

The nervous system is unique above all other body systems, because the energy of man's soul courses through it. It is one of the most vital and exciting systems of the body. The nervous system encompasses the study of the brain and spinal cord. It includes research into cell types and nerve pathways.

The brain is the highest functioning part of the nervous system. Studying the brain helps us learn to keep the nervous system healthy, much like studying the heart helps keep the cardiovascular system healthy. Much public health education is centered around learning about cardiovascular health. Yet there is a void of public health education on the nervous system. I've designed this book to address that public health need.

The word *neurological* describes the nervous system. It is composed of the prefix, *neuro* (relating to nerves), and the familiar word, *logical*. The Oxford English dictionary defines neurological as, "The branch of philosophy that treats of the forms of thinking in general, and more specifically, of inference and scientific method."[1] I am glad the word *neurological* contains enough science in it to ensure

> **Studying the brain helps us learn to keep the nervous system healthy, much like studying the heart helps keep the cardiovascular system healthy.**

that demonstration (scientific method) is part of nervous system study *and* inference. When we make an inference, we think about something by reasoning from one logical thought to another. From this definition we see that we can speculate about the nervous system and form theories from our speculations without being dependent on scientific proof.

Connecting with the Soul

When people have psychological problems, their nervous system can be impaired by their souls. The prefix in *psychological* comes from the Greek word meaning *soul* (psyche). Psychological problems involve the soul. Emotion, intellect, and will are disordered in a way that affects the nervous system. When psychiatrists prescribe medicine for neurological problems that are psychological, they are admitting that the root cause is a problem with the soul. A diagnosis of bipolar disease in the nervous system is, in part, a problem of the soul.

Science shows us that the nervous system is a system of light because it runs on electric charges. (*Bipolar* is an electrical term). These electrical charges are affected by how a person thinks, feels, and acts. Because the nervous system is an electrical system, it has the ability to take in light. Scientists call this process photosynthesis. I am going to show how light is exhibited in the human nervous system.

Experts in the field of psychology will benefit from this book because it offers an interesting perspective on the soul. Neurologists will find it intriguing because I lend a creative focus to science. I intend to make learning about the nervous system as simple and interesting as possible for the general public. I will be focusing on how emotion, intellect, and will affect the nervous system. I will consider new research on resilience and adaptability. I will explain the process of photosynthesis in the nervous system. Throughout the book, I will add points on spirituality.

Where Research Is Leading

The nervous system is a popular field to study today. The most exciting and current research available is a new initiative proclaimed by President Obama in 2014. It is called the *Brain Research through Advancing Innovative Neurotechnologies* (BRAIN). It is setting a promising horizon. President Obama said that the brain is the last frontier of knowledge. He has approved billions of dollars to the National Institutes of Health (NIH) to study the brain.

Science shows us that the nervous system is a system of light because it runs on electric charges. ... These electrical charges are affected by how a person thinks, feels, and acts.

By 2025, the BRAIN *Initiative* goal is to have mapped the entire brain. This will go a long way toward understanding how it works. The research will affect future therapies for stroke victims, mental health patients, and people with neurological problems. It will take some time for the research to be available to the general public. Learning how the brain works now will give you preparatory knowledge to keep up with advancing therapies.

Explore the beauty of the nervous system with me and open yourself to new vistas of learning. You'll discover vital information that applies to your own life.

Chapter 1

Memoir

As a child and young adult, I lived primarily on emotion. I fed myself on it all day and went to bed at night exhausted. I felt emotion so strongly that I was controlled by it. I couldn't express it. I buried it deep inside. I lived in an alcoholic family where the unspoken rule was to shut down any difficult or tender emotion. Denial was the family crest we wore. It was seared into me like the branding of a calf. I marched in line and stayed within the fence. Forced boundaries.

My father went to work early in the morning and came home late at night after he spent hours with his drinking companions, having used up all the quality time he should have reserved for us. We were asleep in bed. He'd collapse on the couch, not in bed with my mother. She was abandoned too.

Still, my mother taught me to love and respect my father because he worked so hard to pay the bills, feed us, and keep a roof over our heads. All the externals were taken care of. Only the internal wasn't cared for. Stifled emotion. My mother tried to extract dignity and grace from the shards of a dream burned and ravaged in the face of two invisible enemies: my father's alcoholism and her cancer.

It got worse when she died. More shutdown.

My mother's death from cancer sent my father into a self-imposed prison from which he never completely returned. His guilt for the countless sins of omission haunted him. He paced back and forth in his mind, *I could have … I should have … Why didn't I …* and drowned himself in his beer, a steady but lonely companion.

Again, he chose alcohol instead of us.

Without my mother around to breach the distance between his drinking and our home life, my father would come home from the bar ready to pick a fight. We were all in junior college by then, trying to study at home. The quiet was interrupted the moment my father's car hit the gravel driveway. My brothers, sister, and I would hide in the house: behind a door, in a closet, along a wall. Like mice retreating into a cranny. He never knew we were there—hiding—from him. When he didn't find anyone to pick on, he would stay awhile and leave. He would go back to the bar.

I wrote about my family in a 1995 journal entry:

> I lived twenty-two years in a family unable to express the slightest painful emotion. The emotional emptiness in our house was a black hole in the universe that was my childhood. It consumed me in insidious ways. I couldn't reason where the hurt was coming from. It was a pinhole leak in my consciousness that would choke and sputter, spilling anxieties into my mind.
>
> Silence was the language we spoke, and in our most wrenching experience, the death of our mother, no one screamed. The thin voice of grief was a hollow, shrill wind through the dark tunnel that was my mind. The emotional poverty I experienced stayed with me into my adulthood. It was a silent raw hunger that couldn't be sated. It was only when I put some distance between my childhood and this groping adult that I realized the true extent of my poverty.

My emotions were damaged because of my father's drinking and my mother's death from cancer. As a consequence, my nervous system became impaired. I was anxious a lot. Depressed. I kept up my schoolwork and sports life, but I was always sad, always on edge.

When my mother initially got cancer, I took care of her while I worked at a local shoe store. When she grew progressively worse, I

6

quit my job to take care of her. I went to all her medical appointments and spent time with her at St. Mary's Hospital in Rochester, MN. When I was in the hospital with her, I felt less anxious and depressed. In the hospital, I was dealing with the reality of her illness instead of shutting off my emotions like everyone was doing at home. The medical professionals at St. Mary's were expressive and kind in the face of our trauma.

I wanted to be like them.

After my mother died, I wrote a poem to assuage my emotions. I wasn't there when she took her last breath. I didn't share the poem with anyone in my family. I knew it would have fallen flat, gone unnoticed, been shamed. The family crest was branded into me again. Another scar.

Mercy Hospital

You never said goodbye when you died,
Your muffled cry finally extinguished itself
In the starched white walls of your tenth floor hospital room
Tin-soldiered nurses marched in and out,

Immune to your fading heartbeat
Just palpable above the ticking clock
And the blank-faced silence of dawn.

I ran to you in my dreams every night.

Death visited you first before me
Your soft hand lifeless against the steel bed
Your breath filling the empty spaces.

I wanted to stop the clocks for five minutes,
In honor and memory of you

But they continued forward along circles
In steadfast assurance of their direction.

A New Direction

I decided to seek a career in nursing. My colleagues began to feel more like my real family. As I progressed through my studies, I was especially intrigued with the nervous system. It was complex and intricate, strong and delicate. I studied it not just for the knowledge I gained about it, but because I was drawn to its beauty.

In fact, I had an interest in the nervous system all the way back in grade school. In sixth grade I spent hours in biology class sketching outlines of nerve cells, their center-body and extensions; the broom-like axon that brought nerve impulses away from the center of the nerve cell and the long-armed dendrite that brought nerve impulses into the center of the nerve cell. They were uniquely shaped, as if crafted by a master artist.

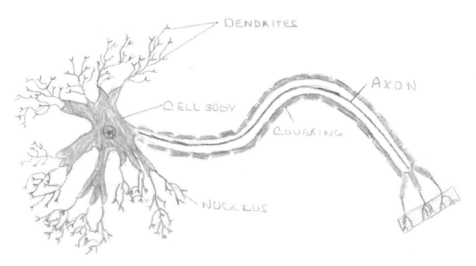

In high school, I did science projects on anatomy. I searched our family encyclopedia for information. When I opened the ninth volume of the 1966 *World Book Encyclopedia* there was a colorful plastic insert of the human body showing the full network of cranial and spinal nerves that began at the head, coursed down the spine, travelled across the fingers and down the length of the feet. The nerves were patterned into a beautiful order.

My college had two clinical departments that focused on the nervous system: the psychology department and the neurology department. Dr. Hadley taught neurology, while Dr. Nolan taught psychology. Dr. Hadley taught about the internal workings of the nervous system: its specialized cells, energy capabilities, and chemical reactions occurring in and between nerve cells. He was a good teacher, exacting in his methods. I was so interested that I attended two classes of the same lesson every week and taped every lecture.

In psychology, Dr. Nolan taught about emotional expression. She taught about emotional illness; how negative emotions can make a person sick. She explained mood disorders. She was an empathetic, insightful teacher.

The only regrets I have about these classes are that, while teaching on nervous system anatomy, Dr. Hadley didn't include any specific lectures on will, intellect, and emotion; and, while teaching on emotions, Dr. Nolan didn't include any lectures on the

It would have been helpful if they incorporated the conclusive teaching that emotion, intellect, and will cause energy movements in the brain that affect it physiologically.

physiology of the brain or nerve cells. It would have been helpful if they incorporated the conclusive teaching that emotion, intellect, and will cause energy movements in the brain that affect it physiologically. It would have helped me make the connection earlier between physiology and the soul.

Chapter 2

Electrical Processes in the Nervous System

The nervous system contains energy that comes from the soul. Most scientists call this energy *electricity*. Neurons transmit energy through electric currents. These electric currents traverse through and across neurons. Since electricity is a form of light, we can say that light is found in the nervous system.

A similar example of this can be seen in nature. The Northern Lights *(Aurora Borealis)* are an exchange of energy seen in the northern sky in certain months of the year. When energy in electrons from the magnetosphere meets upper wind electrons, energy exchanges between them. This exchange of energy, electricity, becomes visible in the form of light. The Northern Lights are an amazing natural energy show displayed in light.

The nervous system has a natural light display as well. The brain, like the body, is made of physical matter. It is composed of cells that respond to energy through an electrical process. When a person feels, thinks, or acts, energy is activated in his nervous system. This electrical process, *conduction*, is a primary process of the nervous system. Chemical reactions occur between nerve cells which assist in conduction. If conduction of

> **The Northern Lights are an amazing natural energy show displayed in light. The nervous system has a light display as well.**

energy is not high enough, chemical reactions are weak and do not transmit effective charges to the next neuron.

The nervous system is a fast and effective response system in the body because it is electrical and chemical. It is faster than other complex activities in the body that carry on slower chemical processes. Isaac Asimov, a premier astronomer, explained electrical efficiency as "an entirely different form of coordination that represents an advance in subtlety, efficiency, and speed."[2]

History of Electricity

A few basics of electrical laws and theories are relevant to this discussion, as they illustrate in a more familiar way how the nervous system works.

No one knew what electricity was until 600 B.C. when Greek philosopher Thales noticed that if he rubbed a piece of fur along a piece of amber, the amber collected small particles (now called electrons) on its surface. Amber is a hardened liquid secreted from a tree when it needs to be protected from injury. These electrons attracted small objects to the amber's surface. We understood from this that electricity had attractive properties.

As the centuries progressed, scientific investigations revealed more about the process of electricity. These investigations revealed an order of how electricity worked that scientists then laid down as scientific laws.

Many scientific laws we use today were discovered by such notable scientists as Christiaan Huygens (1629-1695), Sir Isaac Newton (1642-1727), Antoine Lavoisier (1743-1794), and Michael Faraday (1791-1876). Christiaan Huygens, for example, was a Dutch scientist who was instrumental in giving the world the wave theory of light; that light travelled in waves. His paper *Traite de la Lumeiere (Treatise on Light)* is widely read in scientific circles today. Michael Faraday was a famous English scientist who explained how waves of light are affected by magnetic fields.

It took important scientists like Luigi Galvani, (1737-1798), and

Alessandro Volta, (1745-1847), to continue research the way electricity worked in the nervous systems of living things. In 1780 Galvani was able to show (by an instrument called the galvanometer) how a frog's leg jumped when stimulated by an electric current. Volta discovered the energy potential inherent in that electric current.

Eighteenth century scientist, Antoine Lavoisier, wrote about light, "The combinations of light, and its modes of acting upon different bodies, is still less known, and all the operations of life only exist in places exposed to the influence of light. By means of light, the benevolence of the Deity hath filled the surface of the earth with organization, sensation, and intelligence."[3]

It is amazing to me that Volta, a premier scientist, understood that light was somehow related to intelligence. Let's explore that.

The Soul and the Nervous System

Let's turn our attention toward energy transmission within the nervous system.

Electrical currents are initiated in the brain from mental thought processes. These mental thought processes influence behavior. H. L. Hollingworth, professor of psychology at Columbia University, wrote in his book, *Applied Psychology,* "Two forms of behavior are to be distinguished in the subject matter of this psychology, the one constituted by the behavior of mental processes and the mechanisms of consciousness; the other by the motor behavior of the body and the mechanisms of activity."[4] Our brains are moved by our intellect, emotion, and will. In addition, the soul orders the body to move. The electrical processes of the nervous system have a direct impact on the body.

Sadly, some people live from birth to death without knowing anything about their nervous system. This could be dangerous. One of the reasons I started this book was because a friend of my daughter's took his

> **Electrical currents are initiated in the brain from mental thought processes. These mental thought processes influence behavior.**

13

life. Actually, the weekend of her friend's funeral was also the weekend another young man in our suburb took his life. The ending of two young lives on the same weekend—both claimed by suicide.

James and Tommy were talented and perceptive, young and handsome. James was a gifted musician who could play any stringed instrument, including the Indian sitar. His friends were out to dinner with him the night before he took his life. He never said a word about how he was feeling inside or his intentions to take a gun and shoot himself.

I didn't know James, but my daughter knew him through mutual friends at her high school. She was attracted to his quiet, kind nature and his amazing talent. She invited him to the high school dance the year she became homecoming queen. He declined. She said he was having a problem with his bleeding ulcer. He was struggling with something inside himself. I saw him once after that. My daughter and I went into the guitar store where he worked; she was looking for music books. They said hello and talked for some time. She really had gone to the store to see him.

I didn't know Tommy. Neither did my daughter. I may have crossed his path in the twenty years that we lived near each other. He went to the kindergarten, grade school, and high school in my suburb. When he became a college student, he attended the same university as my niece and nephew. He took his life while he was away at college. His loved ones brought him back to the suburbs to be buried.

James and Tommy's wakes were across the street from each other. Although they didn't hang out with each other, their deaths were linked together. They shared some of the same friends, who attended both of their wakes. When they entered the funeral home many young people almost fainted. This was too much for them. It was too much for everybody. These deaths were tragic, premature, unpredicted. Young adults are supposed to be looking forward to the future. Their life is just beginning, not ending. What went wrong?

No one knows what James and Tommy were thinking or feeling before they ended their lives. It is impossible to know. They were in a dark place, without hope. They made an irreversible decision during a difficult time in their lives.

My first response to suicide is much like everyone else. There is deep grief. I ask the same looming question everyone else asks, "Why did he take his life?" The question can never be answered. It screams from our consciousness, because we live the same human existence. *Why?* is a kind of question asked more to (or at) a loved one who is no longer with us. It is a natural response to such grief.

In addition to this unanswerable question, maybe other questions could be posed that offer hope. What happens to the nervous system during trauma? How do thoughts and emotions affect the nervous system? These questions offer answers and create potential for change.

Basics About the Nervous System

Public health departments do not educate the general public on this body system. Many people take medicine that has been prescribed for their nervous systems without understanding how it works. If they had basic knowledge about the nervous system, they could understand their medicine. Knowledge is power. There is so much that the average person can do to have a positive effect on his nervous system.

Here are a few basics about the nervous system:

The nervous system contains two general types of nerve cells: glia and neurons. When a person engages his will, thinking, or emotion, energy is carried and moved around the nervous system by these cells. Neurons and glia function differently, but the commonality between them is that they both process energy. (Some neurons and glia exist outside the central nervous system, but I deal mostly with glia and neurons in the brain's cerebral cortex.)

We occasionally hear people in popular culture refer to "grey matter" without understanding what it does. Grey matter is the collective gathering of neurons and glia into a mass of cells that actually are grey in color. Grey matter is found in the uppermost layer of the cerebral cortex called the neocortex. The neocortex is composed of six layers: 1) the highest molecular layer, 2) the external granular layer, 3) the external pyramidal layer, 4) the internal granular layer, 5) the internal pyramidal layer, and 6) the multiform layer. Neurons and glia are found in different layers of the neocortex according to their function.

Several types of neurons carry out a variety of functions in the nervous system. They all conduct nerve impulses. Neurons get excited by the stimulation of energy.

Neurons in the central nervous system process the energy of will, thinking, and emotion. This energy causes excitability that starts a nerve impulse. Interneurons in the central nervous system can, when appropriate, stop the excitability, thereby giving rest to the neuron and overall balance to the nervous system. Interneurons are located between a beginning neuron and a terminating neuron. The soul's energy is the light that moves through nerve tracts much like energy moves through electrical wires in a house.

Electricity is moved by a flow of electrons in the nerve cell. The measure of this flow is called a current of electricity. The electric current's overall strength is dependent on the amount of electrons present and the forcefulness of the electrons. This will be critical as we deepen our discussion of the soul in the next chapter.

Chapter 3

How the Soul Affects the Nervous System

Every man possesses a soul. This is a true claim, because it is logically undeniable. If a man says, "I am not a soul" his statement is false, because he is making this statement with his soul. This is a self-defeating statement. No man can deny his soul without being contradictory.

A person's soul moves its energy by using neurons in the brain. The amount of energy the soul gives out is exerted on electrons in the neuron. The energy moves electrically at junctures between neurons called synapses. According to *Encyclopedia Britannica*, "Rapid neuronal communication at these (synaptic) junctions is probably not chemical but electrical in nature."[5] If the energy is a high enough, the chemical reaction at the synapse occurs and conducts electricity to the next neuron. This continues from neuron to neuron. Nerve cells at their basic function are very associational (as is the soul itself). An electrical signal in the nervous system can travel one city block in one second! How we use our soul is immediate and vital to our nervous system.

> **A person's soul moves its energy by using neurons in the brain.**

The Soul Defined

The soul is composed of emotion, intellect, and will. These three faculties are arranged in a functional hierarchy so the faculties can work together in organized unity. Man feels emotion. He thinks and analyzes information. He makes decisions with his will.

Since we are sensation-driven and passion-craved beings, emotion often comes first and feels more powerful than the intellect and will, but in terms of function, emotion is not the most powerful. Some early philosophers believed emotion had control over the mind and body. Hume said that reason is slave to the passions. Granted, emotion has a strong motivating factor, but it is not the highest functioning part of the soul.

Emotion as a faculty of the soul is a passive faculty that the intellect analyzes and the will directs. Will is the highest faculty of the soul because it has the function of acting. Thomas Lickona, a developmental psychologist explains, "It takes will to keep emotion under the control of reason."[6] If a person lets emotion overrule, it can create an imbalance in the soul, and consequently, in the nervous system.

Emotions have low-functioning ability in the brain based on their passivity. We may not have control over whether they are there, but we do have control over what we think of them (intellect) and what do with them (will). Feelings float in and out of our minds when events occur or in relationships with other people.

When something is passive, it is said to have potential. It cannot act. Emotion is the least-functioning faculty of the soul, because it is the highest in passivity. Since emotion is passive, it can only be an influencing factor to the intellect and will.

Emotion motivates man from infancy throughout adulthood. Experts have identified four emotional states that affect the nervous system: love, fear, anger, and sadness. These emotions are dramatic and, when in balance, are enjoyable expressions of life. They initiate electrical stimuli in the brain that culminate in physiological processes in the nervous system.

Excess or deprivation of emotion is unhealthy for the soul and for the nervous system. Too much love creates dependence. Too much fear creates insecurity. Too much anger creates aggression. Too much sadness creates depression. Conversely, a lack of love creates loneliness. Too little fear creates overconfidence. Inability to express anger creates passivity. A lack of empathy creates callousness.

Unbalanced emotions adversely affect the brain's physiology. The energy moves through the nervous system via conduction through nerve cells. Over time, the conduction of negative energy through nerve cells becomes a continuous pathway called a neural tract. Continuous negative emotion can cause chronic anxiety or depression in the nervous system.

In the brain, neural tracts scan long distances quickly. Synaptic clefts and gap junctions are spaces between each neuron where either 1) electrical movement interacts with chemicals at the synapse to keep the electricity moving from one neuron to another (synaptic cleft) or 2) electricity jumps across from one neuron to another (gap junctions). Neural pathways are conditioned by the emotional responses a person continues to experience. This conditions the nervous system and creates a habitual nerve response. If healthy emotions occur regularly, the nervous system can create new conduction that then creates healthier nerve tracts.

> **If healthy emotions occur regularly, the nervous system can create new conduction that then creates healthier nerve tracts.**

Emotional Expression in the Nervous System

When a person feels love, fear, or anger in an unhealthy degree, the nervous system usually speeds up. When neurons speed up, the nervous system is on high alert. Conversely, when a person is sad, the nervous system slows. Neurons don't connect efficiently or effectively, so a person may not think or act in constructive ways. James and Tommy, the two boys who took their lives, may have had neurological problems that were affected by psychological trauma. Their neurons may have been damaged, so they reacted in a way contrary to life.

Dr. Travis Bradberry, and Dr. Jean Greaves, authors of *Emotional Intelligence 2.0* write about how emotions affect the brain, "The affective character of a stimulating situation is a function of the pathway traversed by the neural impulse. Any change of affective tone thus involves a definite shift of conduction pathway, and the theories are forced to account for the effectiveness of experience in promoting these shifts."[7]

My friend had a problem controlling anger. He would get angry easily and lose his temper. He could feel his nervous system speeding. He could feel his pulse race. He wanted to manage his anger better, but, because he consistently had given in to anger over many years, this took patience and reconditioning. Success came slowly after many months. Every time he made the choice not to lose his temper, he was stopping a negative neurological stimulus from occurring, and he was physiologically changing his nervous system! As time went on, he noticed he was less and less angry about things that used to bother him. He was calmer too. As he was getting physiologically healthier, the neural conduction pathway formed from his anger diminished from disuse.

Emotions are processed in the amygdala portion of the brain. The amygdala, two almond-shaped areas just behind the eyes and next to the ears, are perfectly placed. This location allows a person to subjectively pick up cues by what he sees in a facial expression and what he hears in a person's voice.

When a person feels an emotion, he transfers energy to the amygdala. The energy causes neurons to start oscillating, that is, moving in place rhythmically and repetitively. Other surrounding neurons pick up these electrical movements and start oscillating too. This creates a bigger area of electrical charge. Emotion engages the nervous system. Positive emotion engages the nervous system positively. Negative emotion engages the nervous system negatively.

Emotional Effects of Trauma

The worst outcome of negative emotion is suicide. Its intense trauma affects not only the victim, but family and friends, even the community, sometimes for years afterward. Suicide is a harsh act. When a person commits suicide, he tragically makes an irreversible decision during a time when his nervous system may be severely compromised or damaged. (Remember, when intellect, emotion, and will are highly activated in a negative way, the nervous system is adversely affected.)

Suicide has no boundaries. It happens to rich and poor, the educated and uneducated, every race, women and men. It is a family problem that has emotional ramifications for the survivors. It is a difficult emotional time for family members. There is a lot of grief work to be done. They have to process their own stress particular to suicide while grieving the loss of their loved one. Their own nervous systems are affected.

A gifted pediatric cardiovascular surgeon named Hani Hennein was a victim of suicide. His suicide left a wife of thirty years widowed and four children without a father. How did family members deal with this tragic loss? Hani's family reacted with grace, understanding, and forgiveness—healthy components in any grief situation.

Hani's son spoke to a news reporter when the suicide happened, "Hennein's eighteen-year-old son, Phillip, remembered his father, then a Little League baseball coach, once teaching the mantra of, 'don't complain, don't explain … it's the coming back that counts,' after the younger Hennein committed an error in the field. In a way, I know he's come back from his death,' Phillip said. I'm 100 percent sure he's in heaven and 100 percent certain he's overcome the torments of his life,' he said.'"

Hani's sister, Mona, also spoke to a reporter. Her words are poetic and healing, "Mona Oscai, Hennein's sister, said Hennein was a phenomenal pediatric cardiothoracic surgeon who gave his life to operating on infants born with heart defects. 'Oftentimes, Hennein would repair hearts as small as the tip of an index finger. For children all over the country, Hani put fire back in those hearts and his life, like a candle in the wind, ended quickly because he didn't know where to turn when the rains came,' Oscai said.

Oscai also said, "Laughing children across the United States and Africa will live on despite his abrupt death."[8]

Beautiful memories of the loved one can help the grief process. Memories that are painful may also be recalled, but even this is healthy because emotions that surface have the opportunity to be exposed and healed. And, as we have seen with the Hennein family, grace, under-standing, and forgiveness can overcome the negative effects of trauma.

Research on Emotion

The effect of emotion on the nervous system has been and contin-ues to be a fascinating area of study. Author John Dashiell explains, "The 'complexes' discovered by the psychoanalysts are really senti-ments that happen to operate pathologically."[9]

The brain keeps millions of memories that are attached to emotions from these past events. A memory can return to consciousness because it is emotionally aroused by something seen or heard in the present. These memories affect the nervous system, particularly the amygdala. When a painful event that caused deep emotional hurt keeps coming up and the deep emotional hurt has not been dealt with, the amygdala keeps getting negatively stimulated and may incur damage from excess stimulation.

Some experimenters who observe the effect of emotions on the brain by artificially stimulating parts of the brain with a probe have shown that when the brain is stimulated, certain areas light up. The *Encyclopedia Britannica* says, "Which parts of the cerebral hemispheres pro-cess emotion has been learned from patients with epilepsy and from operations under local anesthesia in which the electrical stimulation of the brain is carried out."[10] The activating principle, the electrical probe, an artificial device, begins the stimulation. Scientists have observed the same kind of electrical stimulation when a person experiences his emo-tions naturally. A stimulation lights the brain in the area that processes emotion. This electrical stimulation is initiated by the soul's energy.

Through the centuries there have been many studies on emotion, what it is, and how it is processed. In *The Expression of Emotion in Man and Animals,* Charles Darwin wrote his observations of human faces and their expressions. His research revealed common facial expressions of emotion. For example, when a person is feeling angry, muscles around his eyes tighten. When a person is concentrating on an object or idea, muscles around his lips tighten. In Darwin's time it was easy to do research on the outward expression of emotion, but it was difficult to do research on the origin of emotion within because they did not have the medical machines we have today. Darwin's research doesn't address the source of emotion

Early studies on the origin of emotion were more theoretical than scientific. In the early nineteenth century, psychologist William James and physician Carl George Lange believed a sensation begins physiologically and becomes a feeling as the brain reacts to the sensation. In their theory, the physiological event of crying occurs first and then a person realizes he is sad. Their theory proposed that the cause of emotion was a physiological sensation and the effect from this physiological sensation was an emotion. They believed emotion originated from a sensation felt by the body and was merely a perception of the body.

> **Scientists have observed electrical stimulation when a person experiences emotions naturally. A stimulation lights the brain in the area that processes emotion. This electrical stimulation is initiated by the soul's energy.**

James and Lange didn't believe that emotion was first experienced in the soul and then the soul's energy affected the brain. Today, through technological advances and imaging devices, we can watch a person feel an emotion and see the energy coursing through the brain. People have more control over their nervous system than they realize.

Emotional IQ

A state of high emotion can too highly influence the intellect and will, creating an unhealthy state of the soul, which creates an unbalanced nervous system. When unbalanced emotions aren't controlled by the intellect and acted upon in a healthy way by the will, it adversely affects the individual himself. It also affects communities and society as a whole. For example, unharnessed anger can become violent. School shootings are occurring at a more frequent rate. Disgruntled employees are murdering coworkers. Emotion is destructive when it has too strong a hold in the soul. Emotion is healthiest when it is properly sub-jugated under the intellect and will.

In the late 1900s William Stern devised IQ tests. They were scien-tific intelligence tests that measured a person's intellectual capacity along chronological and developmental scales. For decades, these pop-ular tests created a sense of identity for people. It separated them into categories depending on their overall score. People who scored higher thought they were better than the people who scored lower—just be-cause they were smarter. Companies hired men and women who had higher scores. Society idolized the intellect. People believed intelligence was the most valuable asset to a successful life.

In the 1990s the groundbreaking work of psychologist Daniel Goleman shifted science toward the belief in emotional (rather than intellectual) intelligence as the highest proof of a successful life. He coined the term Emotional Intelligence, defined as a measure of a per-son's emotional maturity. Goleman devised EQ (emotional quotient) tests for measuring emotional acuity.

Goleman found that emotionally healthy relationships are essential for a successful life. He theorized that having successful relationships promoted internal happiness. Internal happiness was more important than how one could succeed intellectually in the world, even if intellec-tual success gained a person a higher job status or more money. Pursu-ing material success was not the best use of the intellect. His study found that using intelligence to sharpen emotional experience was more valuable because emotional satisfaction made a person happier. Perceiving emotion and discriminating among possible alternatives of action assisted the will, so a person could act in a way that would pro-mote emotional health. Emotional health was the primary ingredient of a successful life.

Goleman accurately put emotions under the control of the intellect. Intellect is a passive faculty that, like emotion, also influences the will. In intellectual considerations, thinking is involved. Analysis of events, people, and what to do in certain circumstances is paramount. Disci-pline is an attribute of the intellect because it takes work to study, think, and consider. Intellect, therefore, has some acting ability although it is not as high as the will. When intellect correctly presides over emotion, it keeps emotions in balance. When a person takes time to consider consequences of an emotion, it serves the will well.

Not employing the reasoning skills of intellect, can lead the will to destructive, hasty, and harmful acts. Negative emotion keeps humans in an immature state, especially when they act on their negative emotion. When people have good intellectual control over their emotions, they don't run their nervous systems according to ever-changing and often-faltering emotions. Changing emotions, conversely, would run a nervous system up and down, slow and fast, with inconsistent nerve patterns, which is what we see with bi-polar nervous system problems. I am speculating that this may be some of the problem for this group of people. It is a soul problem that has become a nervous system problem. Granted, this is not true for all people who have a bi-polar nervous system. Their nervous system problem could have been inherited from the generations. If this is so, it would still be helpful for them to use the reasoning skills of the intellect before acting on their emotion. Medication also is helpful.

Bradberry and Greaves, clinical psychologists who develop emotional models (EQ) for businesses, believe rational thought controls emotion, so they consider intellect a higher function than emotion. "You do control the thoughts that follow an emotion, and you have a great deal of say in how you react to an emotion—as long as you are aware of it."[11] Thought-induced emotion can bring about positive change in the nervous system.

Many people believe they can't control emotions that rise quickly, often quicker than rational thought can process. At times this is true. Although emotions surface in most cases involuntarily, they can be harnessed and conditioned by the intellect and the will. Daniel Goleman wrote in *Emotional Intelligence*, "In the early elementary years, students should learn to recognize and accurately label their emotions and in how they lead them to act."[12] If a person works at it, he can form intellectual and willed habits that keep his nervous system healthy even when negative emotions come upon them in an immediate way.

As Harvey Carr wrote, "This emotional reaction is susceptible to the influence of training and experience, and we find that it becomes considerably modified in the course of individual development. All emotional reactions need to be subjected to a considerable amount of training if they are to be utilized effectively."[13]

Many times, thinking thought about an experience creates an emotional response. For example, a young man is thinking about asking someone out on a date, and he remembers a rejection from his past. If the girl he asks says no this time, his memory recall may cause him to feel rejected—when it could merely be that the girl had a previous engagement for that day and time. When he employs his intellect over his emotion, he can understand that the emotion is a feeling and his rational intellect can reason that he is in a new situation and the emotion may not apply. We can see from this that intellect and emotion are working parts of the soul that have an interactive relationship in all our moments: past, present, and future—and they affect our nervous system.

The Role of Critical Thinking

When a person thinks, he creates ideas. These ideas are translated into a neuron response that energizes the nervous system. Harvey Carr explains,

> An idea, like perception, is a dynamic as well as a cognitive process. An idea not only represents an object, but it acts as a stimulus and exerts some dynamic influence upon the general trend of mental events. ... Ideas, like perception and other mental events, are experiential activities of the organism that involve the release of neural energy and hence they must exert some effect upon the behavior situation in which they occur.[14]

The more a person thinks, the more he sharpens critical thinking—an extended process of thought that requires intentional analysis of a problem by gathering facts, evaluating facts, and making judgments. It requires an open mind and the ability to think logically. The more a person engages in critical thinking, the better he gets at it and the more his nervous system (especially the prefrontal cortex of the brain) is sharpened.

Critical thinking is a vital tool for emotions. A person can limit or eradicate his unhealthy emotions based on consideration by the intellect. Intellect is like a rudder in a boat. It can steer emotion in a healthy direction. The more a person engages his intellect, the more the intellect manages emotion, and the more balanced his nervous system. In this way, energy from the soul is positive and useful for healthy nerve conduction (conditioning also ensures strong future capability). Proper conduction releases the right amount of chemicals at the synapses, moves the nerve response through the brain, and lays down healthy nerve tracts.

Biologists and psychologists agree that:

- Intellect is essential to healthy emotion.
- Healthy emotion makes for satisfied life.
- Satisfied lives create healthy societies as people act in mature ways.

Actions Take Center Stage

Acting is the highest function of the soul. Anything active is always higher in function than something that merely has potential. Action is potential realized! Things that are active are a higher function because they can make changes while things that are passive cannot directly change anything. In humans, acting is a process of the will.

Thomas Aquinas, an influential philosopher of the thirteenth century, did extraordinary writing on the characteristics of the will. Aquinas realized the will could freely choose. The will was a power of the soul. It desired the best good, although the best good was often not understood or, if understood, not chosen. During his time, society embraced and applied his concept of the will and considered it the most prized faculty of the soul.

The will makes decisions internally and acts on them externally.

When a person makes an inner resolve to do something, he acts out the intention. The will is the most powerful part of the soul. The will does not influence itself; intellect and emotion influence it. The will is used in simple ways for many of our daily activities, but in complex ways for some of the most pressing and altering decisions of a person's life. Moral decisions are like this. The will is the moral actor of the soul.

The Blame Game

Learning about the will is vital to our lives. We can't let people make us believe we have no control over our emotions and thoughts and aren't responsible for them. An action is a responsibility of the will. If we believe emotions are to blame for our actions, we are copping out. Society seems to be going in this direction. We all need to remember the will, not our emotions, causes actions.

We need the input of the intellect to help our will. We can't forego the intellectual analysis needed to make critical decisions in our lives. Without intellectual analysis critical decisions, if made wrongly, can impact our own lives and those of others around us. We should take responsibility for our actions by understanding that the will is free and makes free choices.

> **If we believe emotions are to blame for our actions, we are copping out. Society seems to be going in this direction. We all need to remember the will, not our emotions, causes actions.**

Healthy Balance

The will affects the nervous system for good or bad. C. H. Waddington, a British philosopher and scientist said, "The difficulty, of course, is that our will is obviously connected with a material structure, namely, our brain and the events going on in material structures proceed according to certain laws of causation."[15] We can understand some of the effect of the will on the nervous system by observing people who engage their wills often. They are neurologically healthy people who set positive goals and accomplish them. They are often energetic, because their will drives their brain and their brain drives their body.

People who engage their will in the healthiest way do not act hastily upon thoughts or emotions that carry all kinds of negative neurological excitations and inhibitions. They often have high intellects because they have honed their critical thinking skills before they act during stressful times. They exercise good judgment prior to action. They don't deny strong emotion but quell negative passions. They use good judgment to deeply affect others in their actions. They have honed their emotions to the highest emotion one can feel: empathy. They do not dismiss emotion or intellect. Rather, they acknowledge vital input from both when making decisions.

In this way, they can act wisely. Their nervous systems are in good order. The neurons have consistent electrical excitation so that neuron firing is successful and the resting phase of the neuron occurs at necessary and healthy intervals.

Will and Intellect Collaborate

The will has an interactive relationship with the intellect. A person who has to make a decision considers the intellect because the intellect collects data, analyzes information, and sums up data. Then the will can make an informed decision.

Carr explained, "When reason is employed, the subject refrains from acting, perceptually analyzes the situation, and thinks of what will happen in case he should act in a given way. The solution is discovered by means of movements in the one case and by means of ideas in the other. In one method the subject learns by doing, and in the other the subject learns by thinking."[16]

The intellect feeds into the will so a person can act successfully in the world. This success plays out physiologically in the nervous system.

A person can make wise decisions when the intellect is properly considered. Every day, we have external experiences and events that we have no control over. You could be driving with exact precision, but the person driving the car in the opposite lane could be out of control and swerve into your lane. You may incur an injury like a torn shoulder joint. More than likely you would have to go to physical therapy to rehabilitate your shoulder. Your decision to go to therapy and do your exercises will determine your success and the health of your muscular system.

Reactions Matter

It is not always an external event in life that causes damage to the nervous system, but rather *how we react* to the external event.

There is great adaptability in choice because the will is free to choose. We must choose our actions well, because our actions can be destructive or constructive for ourselves, the people around us, and society. Carr summarized, "An effective will represents a proper balance between the impulsive and deliberative types of mind. A person should cultivate the habit of examining thoroughly every aspect of a situation, making a prompt decision, and acting in accordance with that decision as soon as practicable."[17] When properly applied, the will can be an iron fortress of the soul standing against life's tragedies.

Soul-centered Living

Just because the will is the highest faculty of the soul and the intellect a more active faculty than emotion does not mean emotion is useless. Emotion is the pulse of life. History shows that passion moves souls to great deeds. We don't have to live without passion, but allowing it free reign can destroy our souls and wreak havoc in our nervous system.

I have the most satisfying emotional life now because, even when my emotions are high, I balance them with healthy intellectual consideration before I choose my actions. Through proper expression and control of emotion, subjugated under the intellect and will, you too can live with a passionate soul and with a healthy nervous system.

Studies on neurology often leave out the soul. They don't believe the soul is the energy the brain runs on. Some scientists consider brain matter just that: matter. They see the brain as just a physical organ.

What they see happening electrically in the brain they attribute to nerve cells and chemical reactions. They don't consider that the energy initiator in the nervous system is the immaterial soul.

My goal in this book is to incorporate the knowledge of the soul into the anatomical and physiological knowledge of the nervous system for a more complete and truer picture of the nervous system.

Chapter 4

Nervous System Anatomy

The nervous system is divided into the peripheral nervous system and the central nervous system. The central nervous system comprises the brain and the spinal cord. The peripheral nervous system is composed of all nerves outside the central nervous system. The peripheral nervous system takes the communication from the brain and spinal column and transfers it to the body. It is divided into the autonomic part and the somatic part.

The autonomic part relays communication from the brain and spinal cord to internal organs throughout the body. The somatic part relays communication from the brain and spinal cord to the muscles. For purposes of this book, I will be focusing on the central nervous system, particularly the brain.

Scientists have categorized three areas of the brain: **forebrain, midbrain,** and **hindbrain.** We'll spend most of our time considering the forebrain. However, it will help to know the functions of the other two areas.

Generally, the **midbrain** is a relay station that coordinates stimuli received from motor and sensory parts of the body. It acts as a filter to process messages from the cerebrum to the spinal cord with such activities as wake-sleep patterns, vision, hearing, temperature regulation, and motor control. It contains various small-but-important structures: the cerebral peduncles, the tectum, and the tegmentum.

- The cerebral peduncles help the body with more precise motor movement.

- The tectum is involved in vision reflexes such a processing what one would see and controlling eye muscles. It is also assists in promoting hearing by receiving and relaying input from the senses.

- The tegumentum has a mass of neurons that work together to promote a balanced state of control for the nervous system.

The **hindbrain** sits under and behind the cerebrum. It houses the cerebellum, pons, and medulla. They control much of the physiological maintenance of the body. This area is sometimes called *little brain*. The cerebellum controls balance, gait, and movement. The pons and medulla control breathing, body temperature, and blood pressure.

In the Forebrain

The forebrain contains the cerebrum, thalamus, hypothalamus, hippocampus, amygdala, pituitary gland, and pineal gland.

Thalamus

The thalamus (Latin word meaning *inner chamber*) is found deep within the forebrain. It is a switchboard between other areas of the brain that helps process sensory and motor signals.

Hypothalamus

The hypothalamus (Latin word meaning *under-room chamber*) regulates such things as sleep patterns, appetite, thirst, and pulse. It joins the nervous system with the endocrine system and plays a role in processing emotion.

Hippocampus

The hippocampus (Latin word meaning *sea horse*) plays vital role in storing memories and recognizing spatial objects.

Amygdala

The amygdala (Latin word meaning *almond*) is located under the cerebrum. It connects emotion and memory processing associated with behavioral decisions.

Pituitary Gland

The pituitary gland (Latin word meaning *attachment underneath*) makes liquid secretions called hormones that flow into the circulatory system during stress, body growth, digestion, and sexual processes.

Pineal Gland

The pineal gland (Latin word *third eye*) is important in wake-sleep patterns and recognizing seasonal changes.

Cerebrum

The cerebrum (Latin word meaning *brain*) is the largest part of the nervous system—the executive area. It is divided into left and right hemispheres by a corpus callosum. The hemispheres are divided into lobes (temporal, parietal, frontal, and occipital). The top surface of the cerebrum, called the cerebral cortex, is covered in grey matter. As we discussed earlier, grey matter (composed of neurons and astrocytes) contains the main brain cells that move the energy of the soul.

Focus on the Cerebral Cortex

The cerebral cortex is full of ridges and grooves that give it a wrinkled appearance. These ridges and grooves increase the cortex surface area so more grey matter can be present. Inheritance factors are one reason for increased ridges and grooves. Famed philosopher Mortimer Adler said, "The hereditary material is, of course, extremely stable, so that it can be transmitted through many generations."[18] Grey matter also increases with nutrients (especially when given *in utero)* and with more activity. Research in Alzheimer's patients show that a person's grey matter decreases when he does not socialize (emotion), work (intellect), or stay active (will). Research also shows that when an Alzheimer's patient is active in these areas, grey matter does not decline. This is proof that the soul's energy physiologically affects the brain.

The cerebral cortex is grouped into paired lobes and according to function. They are the **frontal, parietal, occipital,** and **temporal** lobes.

The **frontal** lobes are found at the top and most forward part of the cerebral cortex where grey matter is present. Frontal lobes light up when a person reasons, plans, or makes judgments. They mature around twenty years old. It is important for young people to develop their reasoning skills while they are between the ages of six and nineteen—the school-year ages. It is a tremendous opportunity to sculpt, hone, and sharpen intellect.

The **parietal** lobes are behind the frontal lobe. They process information received from the senses and relay this information to the brain. Objects, symbols, and numbers picked up are processed in the parietal lobes. The parietal lobes also process spatial images from the senses and are critical to language skills.

The **occipital** lobes that process visual information are behind the parietal lobes. A person sees an object by using the retina of his eye. The retina relays the information such as color, size and shape to the occipital lobe and the occipital lobe processes it.

The **temporal** lobes, found near the ear, process sounds. Hearing and language inter-coordinate in the temporal lobes. The temporal lobes relay information to the limbic system, the emotional processing center. We can understand from this that a person emotionally processes what he or she hears within seconds. How beautiful!

The hemispheres of the cerebral cortex have separate but complimentary functions. The right side processes spatial ability, visual imagery, and music. The left side processes language and speech. A person who primarily uses the right side is more intuitive. A person who primarily uses the left side is more logical. The hemispheres process and share information across an area called the corpus callosum that connects them.

> **A person who primarily uses the right side is more intuitive. A person who primarily uses the left side is more logical.**

Covering the Cerebrum

There are three coverings over the cerebrum. They are called meninges. (Greek word meaning *membrane*.) In general, they provide protection and circulation for the cerebrum. The three meninges are:

The *dura mater* (Latin for *tough mother*) is attached to the skull. It is thickly durable and restricts movement of the brain in the skull. It surrounds large blood vessels carrying blood from the brain to the heart. It also contains smaller blood vessels and sinuses that bring blood into and out of the brain. The dura layer is attached to the layer below it (the arachnoid layer) to provide it with support. What wonderful protection it affords the brain!

The *arachnoid mater* (Latin for *spider mother*) looks like a spider web. It is thin, transparent, and loose-fitting. It protects the brain by cushioning the cerebrum. Fluids cannot penetrate it. While it is attached to the dura layer above it, the arachnoid layer is separated from the pia layer below by a space called the subarachnoid space.

The subarachnoid space is filled with cerebrospinal fluid that provides protection and moisture to the cerebral cortex. It is hard to damage something that is floating. If there is a blunt trauma to the head, the cerebrospinal fluid cushions the blow by distributing the weight of the physical impact. Cerebrospinal fluid also keeps the pressure within the cerebrum at a regular rate. Cerebrospinal fluid is replaced every six to eight hours. (The older fluid is absorbed into the veins.) Cerebrospinal fluid keeps harmful fluids like metabolic wastes, abnormal chemicals, and diseases away from the brain. It only allows fluids that are necessary to the nervous system to pass through it. How miraculous! While the subarachnoid space separates the dura and arachnoid layers, arachnoid nerve fibers grow down into the next layer, the pia mater.

The *pia mater* (Latin for *tender mother*) is my favorite layer. It is the layer closest to the cerebral cortex. It lines the cerebral cortex by folds and grooves. Certain astrocyte nerve cells found between the pia mater and the cerebral cortex work as an anchor.

The pia mater is firm in its protective hold on the cerebral cortex, yet it still only thinly covers it, so it won't damage or suffocate it. The pia mater is a delicate yet tough, mesh-like layer that holds in necessary fluids and allows blood vessels to pass through it to provide the cerebral cortex with nourishment. We can see why part of its name is derived from the word, *mother*.

Perspective on Intentional Design

Scientists use a form-follows-function theory in the processes of anatomy and physiology in all parts of the body including the nervous system. This principle suggests that an object is uniquely designed for a specific function. The meninges are constructed around the most vital part of a human being, the cerebral cortex of the brain, where man's soul, his emotion, intellect, and will, are processed. How tender and strong is the hand of God in fashioning man.

Chapter 5

Medical Tests for the Nervous System

As we mentioned earlier, emotions are processed through the amygdala in the center of the brain. Through nerve impulses, emotion's energy then travels to the top of the brain called the prefrontal cortex. A person starts to think about what to do with the emotion. The prefrontal cortex processes the thinking. Daniel Goleman writes, "A closer look at the neuroanatomy shows how the prefrontal lobes act as emotional managers. Much evidence points to part of the prefrontal cortex as a site where most or all cortical circuits involved in an emotional reaction come together."[19]

When a person thinks, energy is discharged. New and exciting medical inventions have advanced our understanding of how light energy processes take place in the body. Here are a few of these inventions, along with basic descriptions of how they work.

Magnetic resonance machines (MRI) can view tissue inside the body. Body tissue contains a lot of water, therefore, a lot of hydrogen protons. These machines take images of the nucleus of atoms in the body. The atoms align with the magnetic field of the MRI machine and match themselves with the direction of the magnetic field. A radio frequency, adjusted to the atom's frequency, is added when the person is in the MRI machine.

When the atom and the electromagnetic field of the radio frequency match, they are said to resonate. Because it matches up or resonates with the electromagnetic field of the MRI machine, the atom absorbs the energy emitted by the MRI and begins to spin. The tissues can then be viewed.

A test called the Functional Magnetic Resonance machine (fMRI) charts the path of energy through the material brain when a person thinks or feels. These tests take images of the brain by observing blood flow and nervous system changes. When a person is thinking, blood flow is increased to the area where the brain processes thinking.

When a person wants to act, he sends a command to the central nervous system that is processed in the brain. The brain sends the electrical message out to the spinal cord and peripheral nervous system. The peripheral nervous system processes the message and moves the body.

Spectrophotometers measure the amount of energy wavelengths that are absorbed and transmitted. Spectrophotometers measure light energy by a graph that records absorption at different wavelengths.

Electroencephalogram (EEG) records energy in the nervous system. Thoughts initiate energy that initiate impulses that travel along nerve fibers. EEG picks up the energy wave and records it on a strip of paper. These records show that when excited, brain waves travel faster. When calm, brain waves travel slower. When someone dies, the soul's energy leaves the brain, which explains why the EEG records a flat line.

An *electroscope* can pick up energy charges in the brain and show whether the energy charge is positive or negative, and then measure it.

The electroscope is made of thin, aluminum foil strips and a metal ball. The foil strips are in constant contact with each other. When an energy charge passes between the foil strips, they repel each other by moving apart. The amount of energy is measured by how far the strips of foil separate.

Galvanometers can show how a nerve is stimulated and how energy waves move through it. Energy travels over the nerve cell and sparks an impulse. This is a great physiological feat. The energy creates a wave of excitation that is transferred into conduction along a neuron. The galvanometer measures that energy.

Laser machines are a viable form of noninvasive surgery today. Light energy from laser machines can invade the body and repair tissue. The beam of light is full of spinning, fast-moving electrons that give off energy as they go to a lower energy level in the atom. This light is used as a beam of energy that can bombard a tissue and destroy bonds between cells that are disrupting the healthy activity of a cell or tissue.

X-ray machines were developed by Wilhelm Roentgen. They emit electrons that are absorbed by the body. Excess electrons are thrown off by body cells and show up as light in the x-ray picture. Light effects electrons. This is true for the nervous system as well

Computerized Axial Tomography (CT scan) machines are x-ray machines that use light. Light in the form of an x-ray is beamed at the patient and circles the body as a computer records sections of body tissue. This gives scientist a three-dimensional view of a tissue.

Other nervous system tests called Diffuse Optical Tomography (DOT), near-infrared imaging (NIR), and functional NIRS (fNIRS) test the cortical section of the brain where thinking is processed by measuring light properties of the material brain. This light energy from the soul actually lights up areas of the brain when thinking, emotion, or will are active. Much new and promising research will show us how the soul affects the brain.

Medical machines that view the brain can take images through a process called neuroimaging. These brain maps chart neural pathways and show the activity of the brain. Henrik Walter, author of *Neurology of Free Will* explained, "The amount of activity transmitted is a product of the activity value and the so-called weight of the connection, which determines its strength."[20] The charge of the electrical current is dependent on its strength, which is dependent on how active the stimulus is. The more a person uses his brain in a certain area, the more active that area becomes and hence the stronger it is.

Putting It in Perspective

We can see by the invention of medical machinery listed above that light energy can penetrate material objects in the world. Man has a material body so light energy can penetrate into man too. When a person feels emotion, energy can be seen in the center of the brain called the limbic system. When a person thinks, energy courses through his cerebral cortex, particularly his prefrontal cortex. When a man uses his will, energy is directed in the central nervous system and also to the peripheral nervous system.

Chapter 6

Built-in Nervous System Advantages

Strengthening the Brain

As scientists view the brain, they record where certain stimulations have concentrated a collection of specialized neurons. These are called nerve tracks. To create nerve tracks that electrically fire in a fast, efficient, way, the nervous system has to be activated positively. These network of nerves parallel one another. There is an advantage to parallel nerve networks.

Henrik Walter explained, "The advantage of networks organized parallel to each other is that they can process complicated input quickly and are less prone to error."[21] For example, when a person begins to play the guitar, he uses his intellect to learn the notes and chords. He expresses his emotion while he plays.

Scientists have found that people who practice music have localized, enlarged areas of the brain. Canadian psychologist, Dr. Donald Hebb, postulated a mechanism that was dependent on experience. He said, "The more often a connection is used, the stronger it becomes."[22]

So, repeated positive experiences are healthy for the brain and can even hone a particular talent.

An Example from the Muscular System

Most times, we can enhance, even change, our nervous system by willing it. We can understand this process when we see it in other body systems. Let's consider the muscular system. The body has a natural movement to it that is inherent and genetic, but as humans we have the choice to exercise so we can enhance and change the movement of the body into higher coordination. Athletes know this. In Olympic athletes, we see how beautiful muscular systems can be trained to become strong, accurate, and fast.

This strength and agility doesn't just happen to the muscular system. It is an outcome of the will. John Dashiell wrote, "Man's native reaction-tendencies are subject to modification, and that the modified forms become controlling conditions in his subsequent activities."[23]

When exercising, the nervous system works in tandem with the muscular system. The immediacy, accuracy, and strength of Olympic athletes develops enhanced nerve networks in the nervous system. The collection of neurons group together to perform one function and thereby create precise movement. These nerve networks create high firing potentials in the neuron because they have been honed by the discipline of the athlete's will. A firing potential is the amount of electrical excitement passing through a neuron. It excites the muscles in a fast way.

> **A firing potential is the amount of electrical excitement passing through a neuron. It excites the muscles in a fast way.**

Homeostasis

The body as a whole seeks to create balance, known as *homeostasis*. The nervous system is no different. It seeks homeostasis as well. We see this in its conduction of electricity. Conduction of nerve impulses can occur only when energy charges the neuron to the threshold amount of at least -55 volts. The conduction happens within about nine milliseconds.

As energy moves through a neuron, the neuron becomes more negatively charged. After the neuron completes its charge, potassium ions (K+) come out of the neuron to return the neuron back to its resting state of -70 volts. Resting potential is the normal state of a neuron that is not being stimulated.

A French physiologist by the name of Claude Bernard theorized on homeostasis. He believed people have an *interior milieu*, that is, an interior environment uniquely their own. He further believed that this environment always sought a balance. To survive well, a person had to maintain this relative state of constancy.

Claude Bernard saw illness in a positive light. He believed disease was not so much a disturbance as an attempt at realignment. He believed sickness happened when imbalances occurred between the body's internal processes and the external environment. The body was trying to adapt—a good thing. It was successful at overcoming the imbalance and creating a homeostatic environment. It was only when the imbalance continued without correction that it became a problem.

Another physiologist from Harvard, Walter Cannon expanded on Bernard's theory by adding the idea that correcting imbalance comes through a series of orderly steps. He is the one who coined the word *homeostasis*. A synonym Cannon used was *steady-state*. In his premier book, *Wisdom of the Body*, he wrote, "If a state remains steady, it does so because any tendency toward change is automatically met by increased effectiveness of the factor or factors which resist the change."[24] This happens in the nervous system too. After the neuron has charged, it seeks rest to restore balance, that is, homeostasis.

Practical Perspective

How can we apply the concept of homeostasis to the conditions of the soul that affect the nervous system? Our will, intellect, and emotion initiate stimuli in the nervous system that result in either something that aligns to regulatory balance or something that creates an imbalance. For example, when anger becomes hatred, the nervous system goes into overdrive and becomes unbalanced. Emotion heightens and thoughts race. Actions can be irrational and even violent.

Similarly, when fear is excessive it becomes anxiety. Thoughts concentrate on the fear object and become irrational. The nervous system again goes into overdrive and becomes unbalanced.

If a man is a mature human being who has had experience with these imbalances, he knows that when anger becomes hatred, or when fear is overly heightened, he seeks balance by using his intellect to process the emotion through gathering ideas, analyzing, and making judgments on how to act. He also seeks solace and support for his emotions by being with someone who listens and understands. In this way, he maintains homeostasis in his nervous system. He creates a healthy nervous system by the choices he makes.

The brain is the highest regulating organ in the body. Dr. Richard Restak author of *The Brain, the Last Frontier*, wrote, "In most cases of feedback, the brain is the regulator of bodily processes, a point which until recently was insufficiently recognized. Neuronal impulses and chemicals … inform the brain[25] So, when a person feels, thinks, or wills, the brain is affected negatively or positively in electrical and chemical ways. If the person is well adjusted, he adjusts his emotion, intellect, and will in ways that electrically and chemically keep the nervous system in balance. Gustav Eckstein, author of *The Body has a Head*, wrote, "A psychiatrist might describe all of his work as a guiding of the disequilibrated mind back to homeostasis."[26] Dr. Eckstein correctly applied the concept of homeostasis to the nervous system by explaining that when the soul imbalances the nervous system, a psychiatrist can help him get back into balance by having the patient explore his thoughts and emotions so he can act in a healthy way.

Restoring Homeostasis

Homeostasis does not mean that the brain is a static organ, or always in balance but rather that it is always *seeking* balance. Homeostasis in an active process of adaptability. In fact, homeostasis depends on active feedback. A good example of homeostasis is a thermostat set at a certain control temperature. When the temperature in the room gets to the level of the set temperature, the furnace shuts off. When the temperature gets below the set temperature of the thermostat, the furnace goes on.

There are feedback circuits fashioned in the nervous system too. Even during anxious times or times of high stress, although medication can assist, the nervous system eventually calms down on its own. Stress cannot be maintained forever. Conduction of the nerve impulse has its beginning and its end. It comes to a crescendo, then recedes. Electrical conduction exhibits a wave-like phenomenon in the nervous system.

Neuroplasticity

Neuroplasticity also is a characteristic of the nervous system. The nervous system has the ability to adapt. The adaptability is built in to the nervous system from its beginning. A person adapts by reacting to life in a different way that he had previously. Experiences affect the nervous system. Continuous negative feedback systems create neural pathways that become ingrained almost like roads on a highway. Positive feedback circuits can be reconditioned into an unhealthy nervous system by maintaining control over negative emotions that can actually reroute nerve paths. Just keeping away from abuse or neglect can sustain a positive neurological feedback system. An online publication from Washington.edu concurs, "Neuroplasticity is experiences reorganizing neural pathways in the brain."[27] Adaptability is advantageous to the nervous system, especially given the ever-changing experiences that make up the world.

Pruning

Our souls respond to our social and personal environment. This response shapes the brain. How a person deals with events in his outer world, it changes his inner world as well. This happens continuously as we emote, think, and act. The brain is adaptable because it has to process the dynamic soul, which is always expressing itself.

A child's brain is a mass of neurons not yet solidified into nerve tracts. So, how does it change as he grows and experiences the world? Experiences shape it. The soul responds to experiences that impact the nervous system. Bad experiences create an unhealthy nervous system as much as good experiences create a healthy nervous system. A child's beginning experiences is crucial for the construction of his nervous system.

Brain mapping reveals how brains change within the course of a lifetime. This is crucial to understanding how children react to experience and which brain areas are affected. C.L Marvelli wrote, "These maps … behave *adaptively* to the input. It is as if input signals constantly *compete* for cortical surfaces for information processing. The more frequent and important an input is, the more surfaces it gets or grabs."[28] From these conclusions, we can see that the brain is strongly affected by how a child thinks, feels, and acts. The brain responds to the soul's activity by concentrating its nerve cells in a particular area according to repeated stimulations.

> Nerve connections are pruned in much the same way a gardener would prune a tree or bush, giving the plant the desired shape and more room for growth. This pruning consolidates brain connections at the synapses between neurons.

The brain is adaptive from the beginning of life. During gestation in the uterus, embryonic genes dictate growth by laying down genetic codes for nerve cell growth and nerve synapse development. In the beginning, the brain is programmed to respond to instructions from hereditary genetic material.

When a baby is born he has 100 billion nerve cells. What an amazing number of synapses and junctures available for nerve track potential! Scientists consider this a purposeful overproduction built into the nervous system to allow for the later process called pruning.

Pruning happens as a baby journeys from infancy to childhood, as he reacts to the world around him. He is having emotions. He is processing thought. He is making choices.

A child makes choices by concentrating action in specialized interests like eating and walking. The more he eats and walks, the more he is pruning the overproduction of nerve cells. Nerve connections are pruned in much the same way a gardener would prune a tree or bush, giving the plant the desired shape and more room for growth. This pruning consolidates brain connections at the synapses between neurons.

In the process of pruning, microglia (a form of astrocytes), come around the neuron synapse to clean the area, get rid of unused synapses and make space for more efficient connectivity.

Disorganization

Without microglia to clean up around the synapse, the neuron connection is weak and therefore ineffective. Chaotic experiences of lack of effective experience may be the troubling problem. When this happens, a person doesn't fully absorb experiences because there is no specialization of nerve tracts that have concentrated in the area of the brain that responds to this learning. There is an overabundance of cells that are not organized. Experts today are theorizing that a lack of pruning may be responsible for autism and schizophrenia. There may be damage to the microglia surrounding the neuron gap or synapse.

Without microglia cleaning the area around the synapse or gap junction, a disconnected neurological function follows. Fewer neural networks are formed. There is a lot of electrical confusion from neurons firing in differing directions with no clear or straight nerve path. Sociability is affected. Studies have found that animals lacking adequate pruning processes by microglia are more solitary. In these cases, therapeutic measures can increase cognition and sociability which will in turn strengthen nerve paths. Also, there is a possibility of restoring microglia. The good news, as Jonathan Kippis from the University of Virginia explained, "Importantly, microglia, unlike other cells in the brain, can be replaced in the adult brain. We need to gain a better understanding of these cells to be able to better manipulate them in adulthood."[29]

This is an area of research that ought to be studied meticulously in the coming years. The BRAIN *Initiative* may be slated for this type of research.

Finding Purpose

Neurons need to a purpose to survive—they have to be used, or they will be ineffective. They may disappear. Without use, neurons die through a process called *apoptosis*. Choice and action determines which connections will be strengthened and which will be pruned; connections that have been activated more frequently are preserved. Pruning comes as a result of consistent choices a person makes. Consistency is crucial to the nervous system. It creates order that is healthy for the brain.

As pruning takes place, the brain can make space for greater connectivity. This builds a network of nerve tracks into bundles that are united in function. In this way, the nerve firing in a nerve network is exponentially increased and thereby effective.

The nervous system can then provide fast, coordinated, and precise movement.

Resilience

Dr. George A. Bonanno, a Yale psychologist who writes on trauma and resilience said, "Repeated experience of positive action creates resilience."[30] Resilience is a positive adjustment seen in the nervous system after trauma. It is not seen immediately. Trauma resolution takes time.

People who have developed resilience have become neurologically healthy, even resilient. Scientists are finding that around the case of a stroke, the peripheral nervous system grows neuron networks in the stroke area to strengthen connectivity. A lot of this happens during rehabilitation when patients are re-using and exercising their damaged neurological area. The central nervous system does a similar process by sending microglia to clean weakened or injured areas around the neuron synapse.

Paolo Maria Rossini PM, Professor of Clinical Neurology at the University of Campus Biomedico in Rome said, "The study of neural plasticity has … shown the remarkable ability of the developing, adult, and aging brain to be shaped by environmental inputs in health after a lesion."[31] An increase in synapses occurs when a person learns something new. A person who, through choice, creates positive neuroplasticity and maintains homeostasis promotes resilience.

This can be done during and after trauma. We see evidences of resilience every day. We read about the success of men and women in sports who excel beyond physical challenges who are from impoverished and difficult backgrounds. A recent example is Olympic gold medal winner, Gabby Douglas who was raised by a single mother in an impoverished area in Virginia Beach, Va.

We read about men and women who have graduated from college who have become successful in their professions despite and actually because of the trauma they experienced in prior years. They experienced adverse events while they were working hard to succeed and became resilient.

I was one of those people. As I mentioned earlier in this book, I went to school at a nursing program while I lived at home with an alcoholic father. My mother had just died from cancer. I had little money to go to the university where I was accepted so I took out school loans.

I made dinner for my five brothers before I went to school. I succeeded in graduating from a prestigious nursing school despite my traumatic situation at home. I married successfully. This was an example of resiliency gained by continuing to act in the healthiest way possible against the stressors and difficulties I faced. It paid off.

Trauma and Resilience

Long-term studies from the 1970s show how some children were psychologically stronger after trauma. They had become resilient. When they were followed years later, it was found that they had healthy, well-functioning nervous systems. These results surprised researchers. Researchers expected to see that all these children were unable to adapt and had a greater tendency to make desperate choices similar to James' and Tommy's.

This refreshing study proved that most people can and even do resolve trauma. How? When the trauma happened, some children's nervous systems responded to the stress with a surge of stress hormones. This showed that the children were reacting to the stress; they were not denying it. This was a healthy attitude for the child. Their nervous systems recovered more quickly.

Later in life, they were the ones who could work in stressful situations that the average person couldn't. Some of them ended up in the special forces in the military. They didn't just cope; they developed a high level of resilience. They were proficient in coping. Coping became a talent for them.

Dopamine

Another factor that showed resilience in certain people was the chemical dopamine. It was found in good supply in their nervous system. Dopamine is a chemical in neurons that is released when a person feels good after he has accomplished something. It is called a reward chemical. It fosters a healthy environment in the nervous system.

> **Resilient people stood up to the challenge of the stressor, took advantage of the stress hormones that were available to them, and used them to work hard and overcome. When they were successful, they allowed themselves to feel especially good.**

Resilient people stood up to the challenge of the stressor, took advantage of the stress hormones that were available to them, and used them to work hard and overcome. When they were successful, they allowed themselves to feel especially good after having come out of such a traumatic situation. Some people never let themselves feel good after having accomplished something. This proved unhealthy to their nervous systems. These were the few who did not succeed later in life.

Conversely, people who let success be their reward (especially those who were resilient after a trauma) reveled in it. Through this, they learned the value of setting goals and accomplishing them. They continued to succeed. Their dopamine continued to be in good supply. From this we can conclude that resilient people use trauma to their benefit.

Unfortunately, dopamine cannot be administered as a medicine for nervous system problems like these because it can only go into the bloodstream not into the brain. Dopamine is prevented from entering the brain by the brain-blood barrier. This proves that trauma resolution requires active conditioning by a person's emotion, intellect, and will so he can create his own healing. A person cannot resolve trauma merely by medicine.

A person needs to use his emotion, intellect, and will to effect a positive outcome during trauma. As hard as it is, it has bountiful success if a person sticks with it. Personal reward comes from personal effort. Also, people have to practice rewarding themselves for work they accomplish. I know a lot of people who accomplish a goal and move quickly to the next one without congratulating or rewarding themselves. This is not the healthiest way to keep the nervous system in good working order.

Large Hippocampus

Resilient people also were found to have a large hippocampus, indicating an above-average capacity for memory. Memory is useful during times of trauma, because it is a good factor for the critical thinking needed for making decisions during trauma. Also, a person can store new experiences (that become memories) to foster healing or recall memories that may make them feel uplifted. They even can process painful memories that come to the surface. Memory recall is needed when a person has to adjust to new stressors that require new learning.

Prefrontal cortex

The prefrontal cortex (the area that processes the soul's intellect) is increased in resilient people, showing that they are using their intellect when faced with trauma. They are analyzing situations and creating possible solutions. The prefrontal cortex of the brain is engaged. The prefrontal cortex works to inhibit the amygdala during times of trauma so too much emotion isn't processed at the same time; also so emotion doesn't become the overriding influence of the will, above the intellect.

Other Observations

The survivors of childhood trauma also were more likely to have:

- a moral compass

- a faith that carried them through

- a social support system

- good role models, especially primary role models, such as family members.

Controlling Trauma's Effects

How do we as a society try to limit effects of trauma? New school programs that teach children to how minimize psychological damage from trauma are seeing success. They encourage children to talk about trauma so they can work through it. They encourage children to process it emotionally and intellectually. An informative website for this healing process can be found at www.childtrends.org.

Safe and Supportive School grants are available to schools willing to teach resilience models to their students. The National Center for Safe and Supportive Learning Environments have on-line resources available from various models. The website can be found at http://safesupportivelearninged.gov/hot-topics/response-and-resiliency.

I hope psychologists and neurologists alike will give more weight to the life-changing ability humans have to be resilient. Knowing this new information could significantly decrease the number of suicides we have in our communities since suicides occur with greater frequency in times of great trauma.

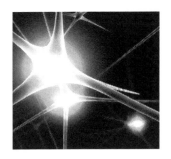

Chapter 7

Pharmaceuticals and Collaborative Medicine

Margene Faddis wrote a book titled *Pharmacology* in which she defines pharmacology as, "The study of the effects of drugs upon living organisms." The older word for this area of study is *Materia Medica,* which implied an emphasis upon the botanical and chemical aspects of drugs."[32] We can understand from the original meaning of *Materia Medica* that drugs were plant based. *Materia Medica* is a Latin medical term that represents the collected research of a Greek physician named Dioscorides who lived in the first century AD, in the time of emperor Nero. His book, *De Materia Medica,* dealt with cures and healings from patients he treated successfully with plants. His book included research and use of some 600 plants. *De Materia Medica* was translated into many languages over many centuries.

European pharmacology developed from Dioscorides work. His years of trial and error with plant medicines laid down the vital research needed to apply the right medicine to the right problem. Despite changes and updates in other branches of medicine, his book has stood the test of time. The history of how medicine came about is valuable to know, especially in regard to medicine for the nervous system.

Pharmaceuticals

Sometimes an electrical charge is abnormal or does not exhibit enough strength to fire or fires too fast. This problem may exhibit itself in anxiety or depression. Mental health professionals prescribe medicine when someone is feeling depressed or anxious, but simply giving medicine to quell emotions is more symptomatic than curative, often leaving the underlying problem untended. The nervous system needs the work of the soul to effect conditioning that can create ongoing, system-wide health.

An illustration of this is the previous example of my friend who had problems controlling his anger. When he got better, his nervous system no longer reacted in an unhealthy way because he had intellectually conditioned himself not to be angry. In any health problem—but especially in neurological problems—a person needs to be involved actively and intentionally in caring for his soul. Reconditioning the soul rehabilitates the nervous system.

> **In any health problem—but especially in neurological problems—a person needs to be involved actively and intentionally in caring for his soul. Reconditioning the soul rehabilitates the nervous system.**

I am a nurse; I am not against medicine. Yet I am in favor of fostering soul work while also, when necessary, administering medicine. Most often administering medication along with nervous system conditioning is the most complete treatment for the patient. This may go a long way toward lessening the amount of medicine needed.

Several years ago, I bought a book from a used bookstore called, *A Guide to the Organic Drugs of the Tenth Revision of the United States Pharmacopoeia 1926, the Fifth Edition of the National Formulary, and a Few of the More Commonly Used Unofficial Drugs. Containing, in Addition to the Brief Accounts of Organic Drugs, A Conspectus of the Families of the Plants Mentioned, A Glossary of the Botanical and Therapeutical Terms Used and an Index of Botanical Synonyms.* It is one of my favorite books. It is a rare book—not to mention a long title. Its title is appropriate because pharmaceuticals require explanation. People who are taking medicine should learn about them by doing their own research into the history and science of pharmacology. Let me give you a brief overview.

From Botanicals to Laboratory Medicine

The book, *A Guide to the Organic Drugs* acknowledges the field of botany within the field of pharmacology. Its introduction reads, "As the vegetable drugs form a very large and important part of the official organic drugs, representing seventy-three of the natural orders of plants."[33] The publishers of *A Guide to the Organic Drugs* were Eli Lilly & Company, a pharmaceutical giant that still exists. In 1926 Ely Lilly & Company had a botanical department. (Botanical departments are non-existent today.)

The change from plant treatment, which is natural, to drug treatment, which is artificial, came about because plants needed to be synthesized in order to be mass produced for the general public. They also could be produced cheaper. In the beginning, this was the only reason natural plants became artificially produced. But later, when medicines became popular and there was great profit in them, companies wanted to procure ownership over individual medicines. (Natural medicine cannot be owned since nature is in the property of the public domain). When pharmaceutical companies procured ownership, they had access to all the proceeds from sales of the medicine. This creates a conflict of interest, which sometimes interferes with their intentions. They want a lot of people on the medicine so they can make a lot of money. Pharmaceutical representatives visit doctors' offices to promote their medicine. Pharmaceutical lobby groups work in Congress to pass laws to promote their products.

Whether medicine is artificially produced from chemicals made by a pharmaceutical company or natural derived from a plant, it can only enhance or slow function in a body system. When a function is increased by a medicine, it is called stimulation and when a function is slowed by a medicine, it is called depression. The degree of stimulation or depression is controlled by the amount of medication.

People who take psychotropic medicine for the nervous system would be encouraged to know that medicine can only assist the neurological processes already present in their nervous systems. This is wonderful knowledge. The information gives patients confidence that their nervous systems are generally well-running systems. I think, too, it would quell their fears about taking medicine. It would give comfort to know that their nervous systems are not broken; instead, they need assistance to function at optimal capacity. Better yet, this assistance may only be necessary during a difficult or stressful season of life.

I hope that through this book professionals and patients alike will come to realize that medicine is helpful when it assists. A person also needs to make informed decisions regarding medicine and care for his own nervous system by conditioning it. This is why it is crucial to understand the nervous system. The professional who prescribes medicine for a patient without encouraging him to foster nervous system conditioning is shortchanging his patient.

Drug Functions

What function do pharmaceutical drugs perform in the nervous system? They assist neurons by affecting the synapses between them that move electrical energy through the nervous system. This is accomplished by a series of chemical reactions.

But what if neurons aren't the problem? A person's neurological problem could be with astrocytes and not neurons. Astrocytes are "Star-shaped connective tissue cells of the nervous system that link nerve cells to blood vessels and, by wrapping around brain capillaries, helping to form the blood-brain barrier."[34] Astrocytes are getting more credit now because new and exciting research is showing how important they are. (I will write more about astrocytes in chapter 8).

If a problem is due to astrocytes, medicine to treat a neuron at the synapse is not going to work, because it is not addressing the root problem. Perhaps this is why there are patients whose psychological problems are deemed, "medicine resistant." The medicine isn't working, because it isn't addressing the right cells.

Medications of the Future

More research has to be done on astrocytes. I am looking forward to all the promising results the BRAIN *Initiative* will foster.

It is conceivable that medicines could be discovered that could affect Layer (I) Protoplasmic astrocytes that assist neurons at the synapse. Research on Layer (I) Protoplasmic astrocytes is relatively new, so we do not know how medicine can affect these cells. New information about Layer (I) Protoplasmic astrocytes needs to be added to scientific research and clinical observation to effectively treat psychological problems that have become neurological. An article in *Scientific American magazine* explains, "Recent research focusing on the participation of astrocytes in tripartite synapses has revealed mechanisms that support cognitive functions common to humans such as learning, perception, conscious integration, memory formation/retrieval and the control of voluntary behavior."[35]

I believe that as more information about the role of Layer (I) Protoplasmic astrocytes in neuron conduction becomes available to clinicians and the general public, it will impact pharmaceutical use for psychological disorders.

If you are seeking help from a counselor and taking medication for a psychological disorder, you'll want to watch this research closely and update your learning regularly. Then you can know more about astrocytes' role in neuron conduction and how these discoveries can impact your health in a positive way.

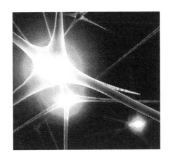

Chapter 8

Light Reactions in the Nervous System

Early on, scientists believed glia (astrocytes are a type of glia) nerve cells were a glue-like substance that supported neurons. German scientist Rudolf Virchow (1831-1902) first proposed this theory. He introduced the glia cell to the scientific world in the mid-1800s. He called them *Nervekitt*. He believed they had minimal function and were a type of connective tissue in the nervous system. Scientists believed him for centuries without confirming his theory. In 1994 scientists began to study glia nerve cells intensely. Today it has it been proven that glia nerve cells are vital, dynamic cells. Their role is to provide support and stimulus to the neuron before it conducts energy. This is of primary importance.

Different types of glia are found in the central and peripheral nervous system. They are uniquely shaped according to their function. There are several cerebral cortex glia: protoplasmic, fibrous, microglia, ependymal, oligodendrocyte, and radial astrocytes. They have interesting functions. I will concentrate my writing on Layer (I) protoplasmic astrocytes since they are so important to the functioning of the neuron.

Functions of Each Type

Fibrous astrocytes are found in white matter. White matter is different from grey matter because it has a protective layer around it called a myelin sheath. Myelin sheaths provide insulation around nerve cells much like the rubber coating of an electrical cord. Cells need this insulation to allow electricity to travel through them. Fibrous astrocytes distribute information to the circulatory system.

Microglia get rid of infection, plaque, and damaged neurons in the brain and spinal cord—especially at the synapse junctures between neurons.

Ependymal cells supply cerebrospinal fluid and help circulate it.

Oligodendrocytes are found outside the cerebral cortex. They build myelin sheaths in the central nervous system.

Radial glia (two types: **Bergmann** and **Muller** glia), in the embryo build scaffolds that neurons use to extend their axons and dendrites. These cerebral cortex astrocytes build long projections out to certain areas in the brain and body so neurons can migrate there. This process fosters neuronal organization.

Layer (I) Protoplasmic astrocytes are the most numerous and functional grey matter in the cerebral cortex. *The Oxford English Dictionary* defines *protoplasm* as "first created thing."[36]
In the nineteenth century, Von Lenhossek (1863-1937) coined the term *astrocytes* to explain these types of brain cells. *Astro* means, *star*. *Astrocyte* means, "A star-shaped cell of the neuroglia tissue in the central nervous system."[37] There is significant relevance to this term since astrocytes light up like stars when they are activated.

Star-shaped Cells

I intend to spend a larger amount of time considering the role of Layer (I) Protoplasmic astrocytes because they are primary to the initiation of electrical conductivity in the neuron cell. I also will explain in depth a theoretical aspect about Layer (I) Protoplasmic astrocytes that is novel and innovative. Hopefully, it sparks your interest for further study.

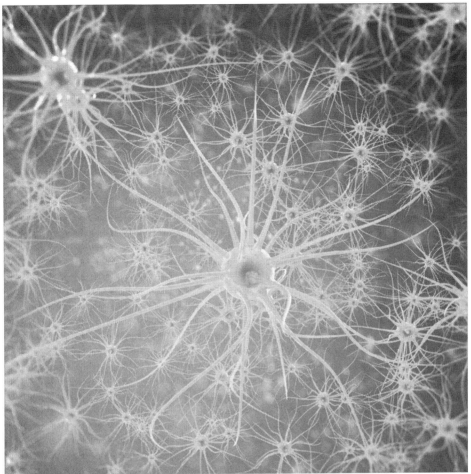

PHOTO CREDIT:: NEURAL NETWORK, BRAIN CELLS, NERVOUS SYSTEM 3D ILLUSTRATION
ROST9, K38030947 FOTOSEARCH.COM

First, though, consider the photo above. This is the amazing and beautiful Layer (I) protoplasmic astrocyte. Just look at that network of cells. Take a moment to appreciate the beauty of its creation before you read on.

Layer (I) Protoplasmic astrocytes are found in the molecular layer of the neocortex. The neocortex is the highest layer of the brain. Layer (I) Protoplasmic astrocytes have the highest concentration of nerve cells in the nervous system, ten to fifty times more than neurons! Students learn a lot about the neuron in biology, psychology, and neurology so most of them see the neuron as the main cell in the nervous system. Layer (I) Protoplasmic astrocytes play a primary role in nerve conduction. They may be the most important nerve cells in the nervous system. I believe recent future research will bear this out.

Layer (I) Protoplasmic astrocytes are composed strictly of grey matter. They can transmit energy by way of electrical conduction through what is called gap junctions. These gap junctions do not require chemical reactions to promote an electrical conduction like neurons do.

Layer (I) Protoplasmic astrocytes do not branch or migrate outside the molecular layer of the brain. They do not join with other nerve cells. They have short axons that connect with cells in the molecular layer only. Dr. Howell from John Hopkins Hospital wrote, "The axons and dendrites of these small cells terminate within the layer, so that they take no direct part in the formation of the white matter of the brain, but have, probably, a distributive or associative function."[38] One group of Layer (I) Protoplasmic astrocytes may have connection and control over hundreds and thousands of neuron synapses! Astrocytes are the presiding nerve cell over neurons in the brain.

Neurons move light energy. Layer (I) Protoplasmic astrocytes store light energy.

Layer (I) Protoplasmic Astrocytes do not have the ability to move light energy. Neurons move light energy. Layer (I) Protoplasmic astrocytes store light energy. This is proven by the fact that these astrocytes do not have a myelin sheath—a covering that other nerve cells must have to move energy.

While Layer (I) Protoplasmic astrocytes don't move energy, they play a vital role in assisting neurons by providing a balanced environment at the neuron synapse so proper chemical reactions in the neuron can occur. Then, successful chemical reactions can continue conduction to the next neuron.

In 1994 researchers realized that when Layer (I) Protoplasmic astrocytes get excited, they release chemicals called gliotransmitters into the neuron synapse. This promotes the proper chemical environment that allows the chemical reaction at the synapse to occur. Andrea Volterra, a neuropsychopharmacologist, and Jacopo Meldolesi, a neurobiologist from Italy wrote, "An important response of astrocytes to their excitation, both by neuronal input and by self-generated stimuli, is the release of gliotransmitters—chemicals that act on adjacent neurons, glial cells and vessels."[39]

When Layer (I) Protoplasmic astrocytes perform their function, proper chemical reactions at the neuron synapse are successful. Without them, chemical reactions at the neuron synapse may not happen.

For centuries, the chemical reaction that caused conduction (movement) in the neuron was shown by the "neuron-synapse" model. Here is an image that illustrates this model. Note that this model did not include Layer (I) Protoplasmic astrocytes.

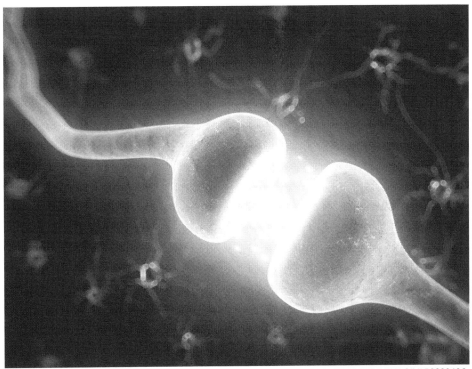

Scientists have only recently updated the neuron-synapse model to include Layer (I) Protoplasmic astrocytes, calling their new model the tripartite synapse. It consists of the two neurons on either side of a

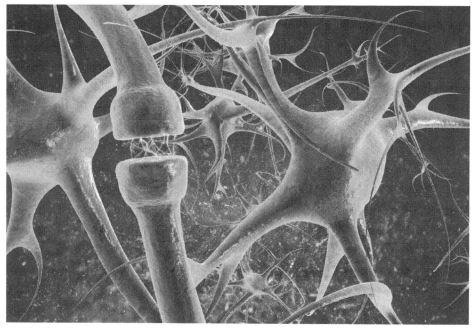

synapse and the Layer (I) Protoplasmic astrocyte along the synapse. In the updated model above, the Layer (I) Protoplasmic astrocyte communicates in the neuron synapse so certain channels or gates on neuron cell membranes open. Only then can light energy travel across one neuron into another. If you study the image above, you'll see the added detail and accuracy of this updated model.

The movement of cells across the synapse continues the nerve impulse through the neuron. According to *Science Direct*, "Astrocytes can modulate neuronal activity by means of release of glutamate, d-serine, adenosine triphosphate and other signaling molecules, contributing to sustain, reinforce, or depress pre- and post-synaptic membranes."[40] Future research will bear out that Layer (I) Protoplasmic astrocytes are equally or more important than neurons for the initiation of nerve conduction in the nervous system.

New Theory on Photosynthesis

Layer (I) Protoplasmic astrocytes work by a process of photosynthesis in the nervous system. What is photosynthesis?

Photosynthesis (Photo means *light* and *synthesis* means *putting together)* is a light-driven process. Photosynthesis involves the synthesizing or processing of energy from light. In plants, photosynthesis is merely biological. In animals, it is biological and psychological. (Animals can think, feel, and act.) In man, photosynthesis is biological, psychological, *and spiritual.* Man is biological because he has a material body. Man is psychological because he can think, feel, and act. Man is spiritual because he is made in the image of God and can think about God.

While plant, animal, and human photosynthetic light sources may differ, the goal of photosynthesis is to accept and store light energy. In plants, chemical reactions process light energy for biological use. In animals, chemical reactions process light energy for biological use and light energy from thoughts, emotions, and actions. In humans, chemical reactions process light energy for biological use, from thoughts, emotion, and will, **and** from their spiritual relationship with God. I will focus on spirituality in a later chapter, as it requires more attention.

All chemical reactions require a source of light energy to perform their work. These chemical reactions happen in steps. Let's look at how photosynthesis works in lower forms of life such as plants and grow our knowledge as we consider animals and finally humans.

In Plants

Plants are made of matter. The energy required for the plant's biological work comes from the sun—an outside source. Plants store this energy in organs called chloroplasts. Photosynthesis is speeded up or slowed down according to the plant's light receptivity. The book, *Biology*, states, "When sunlight shines on a plant leaf, the light of some wavelengths is absorbed and put to use in photosynthesis, while the light of other wavelengths is reflected back from the leaf or transmitted through it.[41] Sunlight can perform work in plants only if plants absorb it. An instrument called the spectrometer can record the percentage of light the plant absorbs, known as its absorbance value.

Plant photosynthesis reflects the basic ability for biological life to take in light energy and use it for chemical reactions. It is fascinating to realize lower nature can harness this light energy from a higher nature as far away as 160 million kilometers! Then, plants can both use light energy for their own biological use and store it for future need—their own, and others'.

In Animals

Animals that are herbivores eat plants in order to take in their stored energy. They can use this energy in their own photosynthesis. How? An animal gets energy for biological work from digesting plants whose stored energy came from the sun. These sources of energy are external. They come indirectly from the sun. The animal eats plants and processes their light energy—whose immediate source was the sun—for its own biological uses. The animal also stores some of this energy.

In addition to the stored energy from plants, animals also have an internal source of energy that comes from their ability to think, feel, and act. This photosynthetic process can be seen on electroencephalograms (EEG) that measure energy waves in animal brains.

In the eighteenth century, a Russian scientist named Vladimir Pravdich-Neminsky performed the first animal electroencephalogram (EEG).[42] His experiment showed that animals have thoughts and feelings that lead them to act.

In Humans

Man has photosynthetic ability in its highest form. The energy man requires for biological use comes from digesting plant and animal sources that have collected and stored light energy from the sun. These are external sources. Man also harnesses energy from his soul. Thinking, emotion, and will create energy reactions throughout the nervous system. Photosynthesis happens in the nervous system. This photosynthesis stimulates a chemical reaction in the neuron that then stimulates an electrical conduction. Finally and most importantly, man can harness energy from his spiritual connection with God. I will examine this extensively in a later chapter.

Sparks from the Soul

One of man's internal energy sources comes from his soul. It is active from the beginning of his life. Through MRI tests, scientists can see light energy present in the resting state of neurons in man's nervous system. EEG tests show electrical light energy too. Mathematician and philosopher, Alfred North Whitehead explained, "When we hear a sound, the molecules of the air have been agitated in a certain way. ... Similarly, a physical cause or origin, or parallel event underlies our other sensations. Our very thoughts appear to correspond to conformations and motions of the brain."[43] The soul processes its faculties of will, thought, and emotion in the cerebral cortex in photosynthetic processes in the nervous system. This is beautiful and amazing truth!

The soul uses its light energy to fuel chemical reactions in neurons. This facilitates the conduction of light energy through the nervous system. According to William Howell, "We may say that when a stimulus acts upon a living nerve, a wave of electronegativity spreads from the stimulated spot and travels in wave form with a definite velocity, just as water waves radiate from the spot at which a stone is thrown into a quiet pool."[44] If the light energy of the soul is effective enough in its photosynthetic process, it will continue to move other nerve cells. If it is not effective enough, it may not move or conduct the energy well. If it is overactive it may move too fast. The soul affects nerve cells positively or negatively.

Biologists first observed and studied photosynthesis in plants and animals. Many scientists today consider photosynthesis in man only by considering how he processes food into energy. Most haven't considered the photosynthesis that is manifest in the nervous system through his soul and through his relationship with God.

As we look further into the physiology of the nervous system, we need to reflect on this beautiful process in the nervous system.

Astrocytes Store Light Energy

The Layer (I) Protoplasmic astrocytes and neurons we discussed earlier are photosynthetic in function, that is, they have the ability to process light. Although the medical community historically has focused on neurons as the prime cells of the nervous system because they have observable chemical reactions that move light energy by conduction, this conduction is the second part of photosynthesis. Conduction is not effective without the first part of photosynthesis, the storage of light energy in Layer (I) Protoplasmic astrocytes.

This first phase of photosynthesis is found in the Layer (I) Protoplasmic astrocyte's ability to spin, resonate, capture, and store light energy. Layer (I) Protoplasmic astrocyte storage of light energy can be used by the neuron for its chemical reactions. Layer (I) Protoplasmic astrocytes and neurons work in tandem to promote a healthy nervous system. One stores and releases light; the other moves light.

Most people are familiar with how neurons move light energy throughout the nervous system, but they are not familiar with how Layer (I) Protoplasmic astrocytes store light energy in the nervous system. Light energy storage in the Layer (I) Protoplasmic astrocyte is not considered as deeply as it should be.

Early theorists believed that only neurons were excitable because they can see nerve conduction. Scientists mistakenly thought Layer (I) Protoplasmic astrocytes did not have excitability. However, according to Volterra and Meldolesi, "Spontaneous excitation is an unexpected property of astrocytes that has been observed in both acute brain slices and in vivo."[45]

By seeing that the soul's light energy is processed by photosynthesis in the nervous system, we can understand that the nervous system is a system of light.

Take note to the mysterious truth that Layer (I) Protoplasmic astrocytes have *spontaneous* excitation. By seeing that the soul's light energy is processed by photosynthesis in the nervous system, we can understand that the nervous system is a system of light.

Resonance as a Factor in the Health of the Nervous System

Within this century, scientists found out that Layer (I) Protoplasmic astrocytes were excited by calcium waves. When Layer (I) Protoplasmic astrocytes get excited, they spin and then move from one cell to many cells by way of a calcium wave (Ca2+). According to *Biology*, "Ca2+ diffuses readily through the cytosol and thus helps broadcast signals throughout the cell quickly."[46] When the calcium wave excites Layer (I) Protoplasmic astrocytes to spin, these astrocytes can associate, harmonize and pick up the same frequency from other nerve cells to join their light energies together. This is called resonance. Resonance is a powerful and efficient stimulation process that gathers light energy together in the nervous system.

The Pound-Rebka experiment performed at Harvard University in 1959 proved resonance between atoms. The researchers showed when an electron moves from its excited state to a lower level, light energy is radiated. This radiation is measured in frequencies—in other words, how fast it is traveling. Certain light energy exhibits certain frequencies. Light energies of the same frequency pair and increase their strength so they can go on to a higher level in the atom.

Resonance is exhibited in Layer (I) Protoplasmic astrocytes in the nervous system. Resonance and spin are part of the photosynthetic process in Layer (I) Protoplasmic astrocytes that helps them collect and store light energy in their mitochondria—mini-organs in their cells. According to Campbell, "The incidence of mitochondrial depolarisations was related to the intensity of illumination."[47] With resonance Layer (I) Protoplasmic astrocytes can then engage at a higher level with more light intensity. There is a strengthening ability that Layer (I) Protoplasmic astrocytes can provide to the neuron. This is essential to the health and ability of the neuron synapse.

Research in Perspective

How is all this information useful? Here are a few observations to help put it in perspective:

1) People need to know about their nervous systems like they know their muscular and cardiovascular systems.

2) Medical and nursing schools need to combine the study of neurology and psychology.

3) The nervous system is a processing center for the soul.

4) The will is the highest functioning faculty of the soul. A physiologically healthy nervous system adheres to a hierarchy of use.

5) The nervous system has built-in adaptability.

6) Medicine only stimulates or depresses what is already in the nervous system.

7) The new model for the nervous system is depicted in a tripartite model which includes Layer (I) Protoplasmic astrocytes.

8) Layer (I) Protoplasmic astrocytes preside over neurons and may be more important to a healthy nervous system than neurons.

9) There are gap junctions between nerve cells where light is the only mode of conduction. No chemical reaction is needed.

10) Medicine does not work at gap junctions. Medicine assists the chemical reaction at the neuron synapse.

11) Neurological machines show nervous system light features.

12) The process of photosynthesis is an active and vital part of the nervous system.

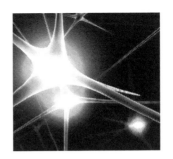

Chapter 9

Spirit Synthesis

Now, let's apply the concept of photosynthesis to man's spirit. You'll recall from our earlier discussion that photosynthesis is the collecting and storage of light energy. On its interior, the soul's energy is expressed by thought, emotion, and will. Soul energy can be seen on an EEG in the form of brain waves. Soul energy is present from the beginning of life.

In addition to soul, man has a spirit. He is made in the image of God. When man accepts the Holy Spirit, he receives supernatural light that gives wisdom to his intellect, and love, peace, and joy to his emotions. The Holy Spirit flows through man's soul and affects his nervous system. The soul is advantaged. The Holy Spirit allows the best development of our will, intellect, and emotion. These faculties then affect the physiology of the nervous system, creating healthy physiological functioning.

There is a physiological happening in the nervous system when a person asks the Holy Spirit into their lives. Physician Rudolf Allers, M.D. Ph.D., says, "The reconciliation of the soul of man to God may bring about a harmony that will adjust defects in the psychophysicum."[48] When the

> **When man accepts the Holy Spirit, he receives supernatural light that gives wisdom to his intellect, and love, peace, and joy to his emotions. The Holy Spirit flows through man's soul and affects his nervous system.**

Holy Spirit and our soul align, we have harmony with God that reverberates in our nervous system.

The strength and vibrancy of this supernatural light strengthens the nervous system in ways that cannot be seen, because God's light is higher than any light man can measure. God's light is experienced in miraculous ways.

We cannot have access to God's light within us without accepting the Holy Spirit. We also need to work actively with the Holy Spirit. Holy Spirit light is present in us the minute we accept Jesus. When we allow the Holy Spirit to guide us, we are in agreement with God's will. The Holy Spirit lights up our soul in active ways and further energizes our nervous system. This is spiritual photosynthesis.

Each of us is a prism of light. By that I mean God created each personality so He can shine through it. This glow breaks out light in the nervous system in refractory light; a combination of colors the world has never seen and will never see again.

Man can accept God's light through his soul. Christ is the light of the world. He is the great light in the faculties of the mind. Miracles of the Holy Spirit occur by His light.

The question arises, then: How much Holy Spirit light are you going to accept and invite into your soul, into your nervous system?

Our souls are not on the same wavelength as the Holy Spirit or God. Only the Holy Spirit and God are equal in power. We know from science that light energy can only be absorbed together when it corresponds equally. The Holy Spirit in us aligns with God and we can feel and know this power. We also recognize it is not our own.

Here is an explanation from scientist Neil Campbell:

> When a molecule absorbs a photon (of light), one of the molecule's electrons is elevated to an orbital where it has more potential energy . . . the molecule is said to be in an excited state. The only photons absorbed are those whose energy is exactly equal to the energy difference between the ground state and an excited state, and this energy difference varies from one kind of atom or molecule to

another. Thus, a particular compound absorbs only photons corresponding to a specific wavelength."[49]

Holy Spirit light is a gift from God that flows through us.

Where the Soul Fits

As we have learned in previous chapters, our will is the strongest part of us. When we surrender our will to God, His will, the strongest power in all the universe, is revealed to us through the Holy Spirit. When a person loves God, He wants to establish and maintain relationship with Him. Having a loving relationship with God improves the nervous system. There is an attractive force of God that draws us in spiritual ways that then affect us physiologically. We are physiologically created to accept the light of Christ. Soul energy is affected by how we build a relationship with Him. We can have His healing light affect our nervous system. With the Holy Spirit light added to our soul light, we can have light in our nervous system that triumphs over life's trauma.

The ancient Greek Galen, the first known scientist, observed,

> Both the attractive and the propulsive faculties have been demonstrated to exist in everything. But if there be an inclination or attraction, there will also be some benefit derived; for no existing thing attracts anything else for the mere sake of attraction, but in order to benefit by what is acquired by the attraction. And of course it cannot benefit by it if it cannot retain it."[50]

Sir Isaac Newton referred to energy attraction:

> And now we might add something concerning a certain most subtle spirit which pervades and lies hid in all gross bodies; by the force and action of which spirit the particles of bodies attract one another at near distances, and cohere, if contiguous; and electric bodies operate to greater distances, as well repelling as attracting the neighboring corpuscles; and light is emitted, reflected, refracted, inflected, and heats bodies; and all sensation is excited, and the mem-

> Galen and Newton, two of our most famous scientists, acclaimed the energy we can derive from attraction to the highest energy source: God.

bers of animal bodies move at the command of the will, namely, by the vibrations of this spirit, mutually propagated along the solid filaments of the nerves, from the outstretched organs of sense to the brain, and from the brain into the muscles. But these are things that cannot be explained in few words, nor are we furnished with that sufficiency of experiments which is required to an accurate determination and demonstration of the laws by which this electric and elastic spirit operates.[51]

From these quotations we can see that Galen and Newton, two of our most famous scientists, acclaimed the energy we can derive from attraction to the highest energy source: God.

Experiencing God

Carl Jung was an influential psychologist and associate of Sigmund Freud. He developed theories about personal individuality. His theories centered on human experience. One theory he developed was synchronicity. Jung used *synchronicity* to explain a matching of two simultaneous experiences that have meaning but no causal relationship. Instead of crediting God, Jung gave man wide liberality to inject his own meaning into events that were coincidental. His word *synchronicity* negated God's supernatural intervening power in people's lives.

Synchronicity is a term that Jung coined from an older word, *synchronal*. He added the ending "icity" to the word to originate his own meaning. The Oxford English dictionary defines synchronicity as, "The name given by the Swiss psychologist, C.G. Jung (1875-1961), to the phenomenon of events which coincide in time and appear meaningfully related but have no discoverable causal connection."[52]

Although he significantly affected culture with his adaptation of the word and his artful theory, Jung's definition of synchronicity differed markedly from the original root word. His word *synchronicity* was diametrically opposed to the word he borrowed.

Historically, the word *synchronal* had been used to denote Christian events and experiences that were connected in a spiritual way. The had a causal connection. *The Oxford English Dictionary* describes *synchronal,* "The things that are found to be synchronal have also a natural connection and complication with one another." and "Those passages in the Apocalypse which, though dispersed here and there, are Synchronal and Homogeneal"[53] We can understand from researching the word *synchronal* that spiritual phenomenon are included under this term.

Jung is one of the forerunners of psychology, which bases many of its theories on a godless ideology. Psychology has to be careful to deny the interaction of the soul and spirit with God.

A truer use of the word *synchronicity* can be explained through experiences that give us deep spiritual meaning. Experiences that have extraordinary occurrences are often the action of God intervening in man's life. This is real synchronicity.

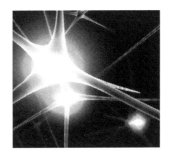

Chapter 10

Spiritual Identity

Most people would say that expression of intellect and emotion together with the will comprise a man's identity. Experts and researchers study intellect, emotion, and will because they too believe identity comes from these qualities.

In chapter 3 we examined the origins and theory of IQ and EQ. You'll recall that William Stern believed in measuring intelligence (IQ) for educational placement and workplace success. In 1995 Daniel Goleman did groundbreaking research on emotional intelligence (EQ) to show that non-cognitive skills such as self-awareness, internal motivation, empathy, and social skills mattered as much or more than intelligence. He believed emotional aptitude was the key to a person's success in life.

Both of these models promoted good qualities for a successful life, yet neither of them fully addressed spiritual qualities. While it is partially true that man's identity is found in his emotion, intellect and will, it is not the whole truth. Identity is also spiritually based. It is a deep aspect of man and without it, he falters.

Why We Need a Spiritual Identity

Here is a story to illustrate the need for spiritual identity. (I read the details of this story in Bhcourier.com. Wednesday, October 28, 2015.

Woman Dies After Jumping Off Roof Of Montage Hotel Beverly Hills by Matt Lopez. In many ways, the story became part of my experience because of my proximity to the events.)

On a fall afternoon in October 2015, in one of the most prestigious Beverly Hills hotels, the Montage, a woman jumped to her death. The news article stated, "Staff reported that someone threatened to jump, said the witness."

That day I happened to be visiting my daughter in West Hollywood, LA. I was at a church service not far from the Montage Hotel. My daughter and I were at the Beverly Wilshire Hotel, in walking distance of the Montage. I was sitting in the congregation when the preacher came out and told us that a woman had jumped to her death from a balcony at the Montage. The congregation was immediately silent and mournful. The preacher extended his service to talk about suicide and pray for the family.

I've often wondered what might have happened if the church services were held at the Montage hotel that Wednesday instead of the Beverly Wilshire. If the woman would have been there, she would have heard spiritual truths that could have prevented her from taking her life. If she reached out, she would have had someone attending to her spirit. They would have stayed with her, listened to her, and intervened.

Did the woman really know what she was doing when she took her own life? We know her intellect was intact because she told a staff member that she wanted to kill herself. She might not have been thinking correctly but she was thinking. We know her emotions were intact because she was experiencing deep emotional pain, so much so that she wanted to end her life. The one thing she was lacking was spiritual identity.

Later that week, I travelled back to Chicago, but I returned to Beverly Hills a few months later. I often walked past the Montage Hotel on the way to the bank. I would look up at the hotel balconies and wonder about that poor woman. Who was she? Where had she lived? How was her family doing? I looked up at where she spent the last moments of her life. I looked out at the pavilion and courtyard. People were eating together. Children were playing around the Montage fountain. Her suicide seemed never to have happened there. And yet, it did.

One day, as I walked along by the hotel, I decided to talk to the manager at the front desk regarding this woman's suicide. A young lady came out from the back office. I told her I was visiting from Chicago. I said I was aware of the recent suicide at the hotel. I mentioned that I was a nurse chaplain. I was saddened that no one was able to help the woman before she took her life. I made a hopeful suggestion as she listened. I suggested that, as a memorial to this woman, the hotel might want to advertise chaplain services for patrons.

Frequent travelers who stay in hotels often feel lonely and depressed. They are away from home and family. They may be escaping from a divorce or another tragedy at home. The manager listened and thanked me for my concern. I walked out into the sun relieved that I had tried to make a difference, that I had remembered the woman's life.

Spirituality is a strong force in a person's life. It can overcome negative thoughts and emotions that occur during stressful times. Spirituality rises above the soul's abilities and gives a peace above the thoughts and emotions active at the time, calming the nervous system. Spirituality can prevent suicides. I am hopeful that in the future the Montage and other hotels will allow church services and chaplain visits.

> **Without God's Spirit, we limp along in life, living a soul life that is not awakened by the Spirit. When there is a tragedy, a valley to live in, we can be defeated.**

Spiritual Identity and Nervous System Health

A big part of man's identity comes from his relationship with God. Without God's Spirit, we limp along in life, living a soul life that is not awakened by the Spirit. When there is a tragedy, a valley to live in, we can be defeated. Our souls can break down. We may get emotionally sick. Author and psychologist, John Bonnell wrote, "More often than not, it will require the impact of spiritual power to bring a disintegrated personality into harmony and integration."[54] This spiritual power is vital to our psychological well-being and to the health of our nervous system.

I have coined the term *spiritual identity (SI)* to explain the spiritual uniqueness that comes from man's relationship with God.

We cannot find full spiritual identity in ourselves, others, or the world. We cannot find spiritual identity in intelligence (IQ) or emotional aptitude (EQ). We will never have enough intelligence or emotional perception to create the highest life for ourselves. Our identities should never just be about how we think, feel, and act. There is a higher plane of being and it is found in our spiritual identity.

SI encompasses God's Spirit in our souls. SI is above IQ because it is not performance-based. SI is above EQ because it is not just about how we feel in relationship with others; SI is fulfillment based in the highest fulfillment one can find—relationship with God!

Almighty God has perfect expression of emotion, intellect, and will. Man, made in the image of God, has imperfect expression of emotion, intellect, and will. A person should be wary of relying primarily on his own soul. His soul should always be connected with God who gives perfect wisdom and discernment through the Holy Spirit.

Since our imperfect wills are fractured, they are divided into either choosing to follow our own will or choosing to follow God's will. To will the will of God is the best happiness for us, even when we don't understand. Willing anything else is willing an imperfect happiness. There is suffering in willing the imperfect, in going against God's perfect plan. John Bonnell wrote, "A sound mind is a gift from God, but the self has to respond to it. As with all of God's gifts it has to be received and incorporated into one's self. If we do, we will be able to go through life at peace with man and God."[55]

Experiencing Peace

We can only find spiritual identity in God's Spirit. God owns, administers, and enlivens us through the Holy Spirit. We may be able to get our emotions massaged and our intellect sharpened in the world, but we can only get the ability to love in the highest form through God. The Spirit gives life to the soul and power to the nervous system. Our emotions are deepened by God's love, our intellects are sharpened by God's wisdom, and our acts are done in accordance with His will. Our nervous system is in a steady state.

There is deep peace in spiritual identity. Spiritual identity works in the dark times when our souls are burdened by life; when we are struggling with an overwhelming event, a difficult person, or a tragic life circumstance. When we depend on God, He shows Himself to us. He is close to the brokenhearted. His love floods the soul and gives strength to the nervous system.

What gives us spiritual identity? Here it is in summary: We accept that Jesus is who He said He is, God in human flesh. Knowing He is God, we can see our imperfection, our fallenness in comparison to His perfection. Then we do what Paul described in his letter to the Romans, "If you confess with your mouth that Jesus is Lord and believe in your heart that God raised him from the dead, you will be saved" (Romans 10:9).

God gives the Holy Spirit to reside within us. His Spirit leads us to seek Him more. The more we know God, the more we know ourselves. Our souls are in order. Our nervous systems, which are affected by our souls, function best.

The Mental Health Connection

Some mental health professionals don't believe the soul effects the nervous system. They think mental health problems are only physical. They believe emotion, intellect, and will are a process of the brain, so they medicate the nervous system.

Other mental health professionals believe the soul affects the nervous system, but they don't believe in spirituality especially not Christianity. They don't allow spirituality in therapy sessions. They believe man has access to healing through his feelings, thoughts, and actions. Partial healing of the nervous system can come from emotional and intellectual insight, but this only brings a person to a satisfied life in the world not to a fulfilling life of the spirit.

German theologian Eta Linneman said,

> The Word of God requires no supplementation, either through psychology or depth psychology or through modern educational theory. God's Word knows man better than either psychology or depth psychology is able to know him. Where the findings of these disciplines contain elements of truth, those were already accessible long ago in God's Word. For the most part, however, psychology and depth psychology possess an anti-Christian character and stand in opposition to God's Word.[56]

It is unfortunate that many mental health professionals miss the spiritual healing they could provide to their patients. According to Donald Tweedie, "To neglect the true spiritual nature of man, and to neglect his transcendent reference, is to fail in the true vocation of therapy."[57]

Psychologists rarely talk about spiritual insight gained from SI. They talk about insight gained from IQ or EQ. Sadly, they don't know the revealing God of the Old and New Testament, the healing power of Jesus, or the counsel of the Holy Spirit.

Freud, the father of psychology, was an atheist. He developed theories on how the mind worked. He left spiritually out altogether. In fact, he ridiculed faith. In his book, *The Future of an Illusion,* he says, "Religious doctrines…are all illusions, they do not admit of proof, and no one can be compelled to consider them as true or believe in them."[58]

Freud, the father of psychology, was an atheist. He developed theories on how the mind worked. He left spiritually out altogether. In fact, he ridiculed faith.

It is sad that the great scientist, Freud, being the great researcher that the world claimed him to be, did not research all religious doctrines in order to come up with his conclusion that religious doctrines were all illusions. Did Freud visit all the tribes in the world, even those in remote jungles? Did he travel back in history to the time of the Essenes who saved for posterity some of their religious doctrines in the prized documents we now call the Dead Sea Scrolls? No.

Freud's statement is obviously false, because there is no such thing as proof in regard to any religious doctrine. Faith is a belief experience in and of itself. Freud's followers believe (have faith in) what he said. This in and of itself would be considered a religious doctrine. The only faith Freud had was faith in his own beliefs, and he was persuasive at peddling them to others as if they were proven facts.

Let's face it; psychology is a speculative science.

Based on Freud's rejection of any religion, he could not provide spiritual help to his patients. He left out any research on the effect of spiritual healing for people with psychological problems.

Science and Spirituality

Some scientists think they have to deny the spiritual reality of God in the interest of science. This wasn't true in the past with some of our most famous scientists who gave us the most reliable scientific laws and theorems that are still used today.

Let me give you examples of how their profession and their personal faith intersected.

William Harvey, (1578-1657), called the father of modern physiology, was physician to King James I who commissioned the translation of the Old and New Testament into English. Harvey also was a respected friend and guest to Jesuit priests in Rome. Yet he remained a scientist. He discovered how blood circulated throughout the body by studying the motions of the heart and blood. He was a dedicated scientist proficient in the philosophies.

He read Cicero and St. Augustine. According to historian Mortimer Adler, "William Harvey was thoroughly familiar with the Bible."[59]

Blaise Pascal, the famed mathematician of the 1600s, invented the first calculating machine and was the founder of hydrodynamics. He developed the theory of probability used today. In 1654 Blaise Pascal had a conversion experience in which he said, "He knew, 'the God of Abraham, the God of Isaac, the God of Jacob,' and that he resolved, 'total submission to Jesus Christ...'"[60]

He wrote in his book *Pensees*, "Scripture says that God is a hidden God, and that, since the corruption of nature, he has left men in a darkness from which they can escape only through Jesus Christ, without whom all communion with God is cut off."[61] Blaise Pascal's widely accepted math formulas are relied on today. His conversion experience is recounted in *The Great Books of the Western World*.

Robert Boyle, a contemporary of Pascal's, was a chemist credited with one of the most important laws in chemistry: Boyle's Law. He discovered that the pressure and volume of a gas are inversely proportional and remain constant as long as the temperature is consistent in a closed system. He was an expert in the scientific method. He was educated and received his degree in England. He was both a scientist and a practicing Christian interested in the spread of Christianity in the East. He gave large amounts of money to missionary work. His work included translating the Bible into various languages.

Leonhard Euler (1707-1783), is another famed mathematician and physicist. You see his name in the accepted math theorems called, "Euler's function," "Euler's equation," and "Euler's formula." He completed a large number of studies on the nature of sound and held the physiology post at the Russian Academy of Sciences in St. Petersburg.

In 1741 Euler moved to Germany. Once he was established there, Frederick the Great of Prussia asked him to teach at the Berlin Academy and to tutor his niece, princess of the German province of Anhalt-Dessua. Most of what he taught this German princess is found in Euler's book, *Letters of Euler to a German Princess*. Quotes from this book show that Euler was a devout Christian who believed in the Divine Inspiration of the Bible.

Michael Faraday (1791-1867) was famous for his studies in electrolytic decomposition and experiments in electromagnetism. The field of electricity is based on Faradays Laws. His work in the field of science was sought out by business and industry leaders. His scientific works led to the invention of the electric motor. Faraday was a Christian elder in the Presbyterian denomination. He made a "formal declaration of faith at thirty."[62] His scientific works that the world depends on today reflect the unity of God and nature.

William Whewell (1794-1866), a naturalist philosopher, studied optical properties of minerals and is famous in mathematics for the Whewell equation. He became Master of Trinity College in Cambridge. The Earl of Bridgewater commissioned him and other scientists of the time to write for *The Bridgewater Treatise*. Whewell also wrote a book called, *"Astronomy and General Physics with a Reference to Natural Theology."* It explained how God manifests Himself in His creation.

Edward Morley (1838-1923) was famed in chemistry and physics. He showed that light travels at a constant speed. His famous experiment was called the, Michelson-Morley experiment, that showed the motion of light was not dependent on any substance in air. This proved that light did not need a medium to travel through. Edward Morley's work ushered in Albert Einstein's Theory of Relativity. He was a professor of Chemistry at Cleveland Medical College. He collected a vast library of periodicals about chemistry that are collected and preserved in Cleveland, Ohio, at Case Western Reserve University. This brilliant man also was a Christian. He attended the well-known Andover Theological Seminary and preached at a small country parish in Ohio.

Ernest Rutherford (1871-1937) won a scholarship to the Cambridge University at age twenty-four. He was an expert physicist who discovered the orbit of atoms and the half-life of radioactive substances. He and his men were the first scientists to split the atom. He also was known to sing the song, *Onward Christian Soldiers,* throughout his work day in the Cavendish Cambridge Laboratory.

Lisa Meitner (1878-1968) was a physicist extraordinaire on the team of scientists that discovered nuclear fission. She received her doctoral degree at the University of Vienna and practiced physics at the Kaiser Wilhelm Institute for Chemistry, among other places. She was awarded many scientific prizes including the Enrico Fermi Award. She was Jewish by nationality and completed her faith by becoming a Christian in 1908.

Sir Arthur Eddington (1882-1944) was an astrophysicist and mathematician presiding over astronomy at Cambridge University from 1913 until his death. He wrote many books that still are read today for their scientific truths. Eddington was a Christian Quaker. He lectured at the Society of Friends Quaker meetings in Pennsylvania and is credited with saying, "The beginning (of life) seems to present insuperable difficulties unless we agree to look on it as frankly supernatural."[63] He was a famous scientist who believed science was limited in being able to grasp the full extent of the world that God created.

Otto Warburg (1883-1970) was a physician and a leading biochemist who studied cell biology at the Kaiser Institute in Germany. His doctorate in chemistry established his revolutionary theory on the cause of cancer. He was nominated several times for the Nobel Prize in physiology and won it in 1931. Otto Warburg's father was from the Jewish Warburg family of German bankers. About half of his father's family were Jewish Christians. Otto Warburg's mother was from a family of bankers from the Protestant faith. Otto was a self-professed Christian.

The list goes on and on of famed scientists who laid down the foundational laws modern scientists rely on today. Their faith in God was not contrary to their scientific laws. Their knowledge of the world and their faith in God were in harmony.

Spiritual Identity and the Nervous System

Without spiritual identity, the soul, loving itself first, wants the emotions to reign supreme so the person can have his desires fulfilled. This is not the healthiest way to live or to run a nervous system. Unchecked passion often creates problems. Those of us who accept our spiritual identity in Christ become what is called, "born again." In choosing to be born again, we are choosing to love and obey God above our souls. This becomes the primary attitude of the soul. Spirit reigns over the soul. The attitude of self-love becomes secondary.

This is advantageous to our nervous system. Spiritual identity gives the highest strength possible to the nervous system, because it is given by God Who is the most powerful energy in the world. Since the nervous system is a system of light, man has the capacity to accept God's light. God's love is full of light. It is higher than any light we have within our soul or within the world itself. Love of God affords amazing calm in the soul that steadies the nervous system. In the highest of saints, there is an abounding love. For example, while Apostle Paul is in jail, suffering for giving the Gospel to others, he is calm and at peace. The martyr Stephen is full of forgiveness for his enemies as they are stoning him to death. He has joy as he looks up to heaven before dying. Love of God gives him deep joy that may even have lessened his pain. Love of God is higher than the soul's love for itself.

Spiritual Identity and Strongholds

Spiritual identity in Christ offers deep solutions to the deep issues of the soul. Donald Tweedie's experience as a psychologist taught him that, "This recognition of the spiritual nature of man, in contrast to the theory that man's activity is the automatic expression of instinctive drives, may well be a revolutionary factor in modern mental health prophylaxis, and psychotherapy."[64] A man who works on his soul when dealing with an emotional problem expresses his feelings, analyzes situations, and decides the best solution. In addition, he prays to God Who gives revelation and insight.

This happened recently in my life:

I spent the major part of my life living under my dad's alcoholism. I never understood the spiritual hold he was under, although I felt its burden. He was an alcoholic for sixty years of his life. He quit drinking at eighty years old. When my father was eighty-two years old he had his first stroke. I was reluctant to take care of him. I was angry that I had to care for him when he didn't emotionally care for me as a child. I cared for him through obedience, because I was thankful for what God did in my life. Eight years have passed and I am still taking care of him. It has been both a blessing and a burden.

He is now ninety years old and in good physical health. He stills walks and drives a car. He has a clear mind. When I was a child, I was neglected because He was an absentee father, but now that I am present with him, he insults me in deep ways.

I am still the scapegoat to his problems. He tries to push his problems on my back to avoid owning them himself. When I was younger, I assumed his problems and took them on myself. Now, I deal straightforwardly with him. I reject his insulting comments. He doesn't affect me like when I was a child. This is very healing. The healing didn't come all at once, but it was worth waiting for.

There were stages to the healing. In the beginning, I angrily called my father out on his insults. I realized when I did this I was not honoring him. This made me feel worse. Second, I wanted to be faithful to God and I knew that His leading in my life would bring me to a good place; so instead of remaining angry, I would tell my father he hurt me and ask him to stop. He would be silent. Sometimes he would deny it. He never apologized. For a while, the insults would end. But then, it would be another day and another time together and he was at it again. Eventually, I realized it was no use telling him.

The third stage in my healing was a stage was forgiveness. I learned to forgive my dad. I see God's Holy Spirit helping me as I forgive him. I stay with him when he insults me.

Last week I started wondering why my dad insults me. I thought that maybe he wants what I have—belief in God—but isn't claiming it as his own yet. I thought that he was jealous of my success and my peace, although it is available to him if he would simply choose it.

Things started getting clearer ton a Saturday as I rested in God.

God, my Father, showed me how much He loves me; how much He approves of me. His Spirit washed over me in such a protective, peaceful way.

On Sunday, I took my dad to a restaurant to meet my friend and her mom. When my friend met my dad, she lauded over how much her mom loved me. My dad blurted out, "Yeah, well, I hate her." In a way I knew he was kidding, and in another way it was a put-down. He said this in front of a number of people who were waiting in the lobby. I felt the comment slide off my back. Forgiveness was working in me.

Beautiful epiphanies came to me on Monday. One was that my mom was such a tender, forgiving person but she had terrible boundaries. She let him abuse her. My dad was awful to her. He didn't help her around the house. He didn't spend time with her. She cleaned inside the house and still had to shovel the snow and mow the grass.

The following Monday, I picked up my dad for breakfast. When the waitress came over to get our order, I said I didn't know what I wanted yet. My dad chimed in with his usual insults. He said to the waitress, "That ain't nothing new. She never knows what she wants."

I remained quiet in my spirit.

Our friend Henry came over to sit with us. Then our friend, Jane. The four of us were having a good time when my dad said something in conversation that was very attacking. It came out of the blue. It wasn't related to any subject we were talking about. He first slung an insult at me and then he said, "You are blocked. You have a block. I have it and you're going to have it. It's hereditary."

God's Spirit guided me as I responded to him. I quickly said, "No, I don't. I don't have a block. I have Jesus Christ. Do you have Jesus Christ?" The abuse ended and the insults immediately stopped. I was amazed that I brought up Jesus Christ in the middle of the insult he was slinging at me. I was amazed at how insistent my father was at trying to pushing his problem on to me. It was great confirmation to all that God had revealed days before.

All these years I felt my father's oppression and now, revelation! What my father calls a hereditary block is a spiritual stronghold that he has lived under his whole life. Two weeks ago, he told my brother and me that when he was a child, a priest gave him his report card for the year and said he was "subnormal." He would say this to my dad at different times during his growing years. When my father grew up and became a Marine, his mom insisted he go to the rectory and visit this priest, not knowing what my dad suffered as a child. My dad didn't want to go, but he loved his mom so much that he went to see the priest. When he knocked on the priest's door in his proud Marine uniform, the priest saw him and shut the door on him.

A few years later, when my dad was wanted to marry my mother at the church, this priest refused to marry him! He had to get another priest to officiate at his wedding. How sad! I don't know what the problem was with this priest, but he was obviously out of line. Teachers have a strong psychological influence on a growing child's mind. My dad has had this spiritual hold over him all this time.

I continue to be patient and forgive my dad. He has had many opportunities for spiritual healing. He has the opportunity to go to a wonderful church in the area where the men pray in groups and talk about their lives. He went a few times and then stopped going. Will my dad accept or refuse spiritual healing in his late years? I don't know. I do know that God keeps reaching out to him. As much as I feel sorry for him, I know he chooses to live under his spiritual stronghold.

> **My final stage in my relationship with my father has been to love him and pray for him. I know God will use my love and prayers for my dad as he used my grandmother's love and prayers for**

God protected me from my father's alcoholism and despair through special people in my life who brought me closer to God.

My grandmother knew my father was an alcoholic. She prayed for her family every day for sixty years. Also, my spiritual mentor, Father Hartigan, the priest who married my father and mother, was a psychologist who gave me spiritual understanding in my teen years. My aunt gave me beautiful spiritual books on spiritual greats such as

Thomas Merton, Augustine and C.S. Lewis. I read them all. I received my Masters in Theology later in my life. Recently, I was chosen as a chaplain at a small hospital in Illinois.

Thankfully, I am not under my father's headship any more. I am under Christ's headship. I have a peace I have never experienced before. I am not anxious or depressed. I am filled with deep joy. Can you imagine how beautiful my nervous system looks! How much light there is in it! I can!

My final stage in my relationship with my father has been to love him and pray for him. I know God will use my love and prayers for my dad as he used my grandmother's love and prayers for me.

Our Stories

I hope through reading this book you can include spirituality in your understanding of the soul and experience the beauty that spirituality can effect in your nervous system. Author Donald Tweedie wrote, "Logotherapy, as a true psychotherapy 'of the spirit,' attempts to call upon the spiritual in man in order to re-establish most effectively good mental health and successful personal living."[65] Live in God's spirit today!

Many people don't live their lives in the here and now. They mistakenly try to live too much for heaven, knowing they are already saved in Jesus. While I understand their wondrous hope and expectation, they miss the opportunity to express the blessed gift of spiritual identity God gave them for their time on earth now.

Our spiritual identity starts here. We play it out as we live the days God has destined for us. Spiritual healing promotes neurological healing. Spiritual identity completes man so much that, though he is still fallen here on earth, his soul is healed in Christ, now! Healing is available in His Spirit now, even as his soul remains imperfect.

We don't have to be in a rush to be fixed. We don't have to be ashamed of where we are in our lives. God is with His suffering people. Many times He works through them more than with people living independent lives away from Him. We can share our stories while we are growing. There is great drama in our life that will give glory to God. We have to allow others to be with us as we grow. This requires vulnerability. In God's hands vulnerability is strength, not weakness; He uses it in mighty ways. He uses us during sickness, and even in times of mental distress.

It is important to share our stories, our pain, our sadness, and our healing in the face of great wounding. If I didn't hear about James' or Tommy's wounded life, I wouldn't have written this book. In a way, a very true and strong way, my interest in the nervous system was impassioned by them. I wish I could have shared the information in this book with James, Tommy, and the anonymous woman at the Montage hotel. Their lives may have had a different outcome.

God is understanding of people who take their lives. We know He understands because of what He did on the Cross. Think about it. Jesus said Himself that He was laying down (giving up) His own life. In John 10:14-15, Jesus is quoted as saying, "I am the good shepherd. I know my own and my own know me, just as the Father knows me and I know the Father; and I lay down my life for the sheep."

I am not condoning suicide. Suicide denies the work that Jesus did on the Cross. Suicide is a plagiarism and a perversion of God's will for life. No one has the authority to take his own life. Only Jesus can take his life because He is God and He can take it up again, which He did in the resurrection. His resurrection breaks spiritual strongholds. In John 10:18, he explains, "No one takes it from me, but I lay down my life of my own accord. I have authority to lay it down, and I have authority to take it up again. This charge I have received from my Father."

Man cannot break spiritual strongholds. Committing suicide can never break a spiritual stronghold. A person who is considering suicide needs to cling to Jesus in his or her time of desperation. He has the power from God in heaven to destroy evil. We cannot. If we try to come up against evil without God, it could destroy us.

My story of a troubled childhood was the impetus for this book. My pain and my healings are now a gift I can offer to others. I can share my spiritual gifts, given to me through the Holy Spirit. We can impact one another so profoundly by sharing not only the joy of our healings but also the suffering of our traumas so that our wounds can become scars and our scars become triumphs. I am scarred by my childhood branding, but it is a beautiful scar. I hope when people look at it, they see bravery, healing, survival.

We are meant to meet certain people to give them what we have. Consequently, they give us something we need. It is a mysterious exchange that brings healings in ways we never expected. Our gifts are our joyful burden. They are not meant to be kept as our gift solely. Gifts are meant to be given. We can't enjoy our own healing while dismissing others pain. This is irresponsible, even tragic.

I love to hear people's stories about the particular times, events, and relationships of their lives. Each story is so intricate, detailed, and inextricably individual. Our experiences and choices can affect our nervous system and make it a beautiful system of light.

Lord, help us be faithful to the healing work You accomplish in us. May we offer it extravagantly to others.

> **We can impact one another so profoundly by sharing not only the joy of our healings but also the suffering of our traumas so that our wounds can become scars and our scars become triumphs.**

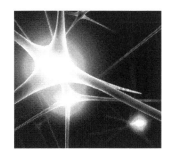

Addendum

Truths to Examine and Hold Firm

The nervous system is a system of light. It cannot thrive without light. The nervous system is naturally equipped with the light of the soul given when God created each person. This is the first birth. When a person accepts the Holy Spirit, it is called a second birth or being born again. The Holy Spirit then gives spiritual light.

The nervous system is surely a system of light, equipped to take in the light of God! There are powerful Scripture verses that speak of the light that triumphs over darkness: the darkness of the world, the darkness of sin in our souls without light. This darkness can become resident in our nervous system, affecting its very cells. Conduction can be ineffective and create chronic problems.

Let's hear the words of the Scriptures, both from the lips of Old Testament saints and from Jesus Himself during His earthly ministry. These words can give spiritual light to our souls:

- He uncovers the deeps out of darkness and brings deep darkness to light (Job 12:22).

- You will decide on a matter, and it will be established for you, and light will shine on your ways (Job 22:28).

- For it is you who light my lamp; the Lord my God lightens my darkness (Psalm 18:28).

- The precepts of the Lord are right, rejoicing the heart; the commandment of the Lord is pure, enlightening the eyes (Psalm 19:8).

- The Lord is my light and my salvation; whom shall I fear? The Lord is the stronghold of my life; of whom shall I be afraid (Psalm 27:1)?

- For with you is the fountain of life; in your light do we see light (Psalm 36:9).

- Send out your light and your truth; let them lead me; let them bring me to your holy hill and to your dwelling (Psalm 43:3).

- You are clothed with splendor and majesty, covering yourself with light as with a garment, stretching out the heavens like a tent (Psalm 104:1-2).

- Light dawns in the darkness for the upright; he is gracious, merciful, and righteous (Psalm 112:4).

- Your word is a lamp to my feet and a light to my path (Psalm 119:105).

- If I say, "Surely the darkness shall cover me, and the light about me be night, even the darkness is not dark to you; the night is bright as the day, for darkness is as light with you (Psalm 139:11-12).

- Then I saw that there is more gain in wisdom than in folly, as there is more gain in light than in darkness (Ecclesiastes 2:13).

- The people who walked in darkness have seen a great light; those who dwelt in a land of deep darkness, on them has light shined (Isaiah 9:2).

- You are the light of the world. A city set on a hill cannot be hidden. Nor do people light a lamp and put it under a basket, but on a stand, and it gives light to all in the house. In the same way, let your light shine before others, so that they may see your good works and give glory to your Father who is in heaven (Matthew 5:14-16).

- For nothing is hidden except to be made manifest; nor is anything secret except to come to light (Mark 4:22).

- All things were made through him, and without him was not any thing made that was made. In him was life, and the life was the light of men. The light shines in the darkness, and the darkness has not overcome it (John 1:3-5).

- There was a man sent from God, whose name was John. He came as a witness, to bear witness about the light, that all might believe through him. He was not the light, but came to bear witness about the light. The true light, which enlightens everyone, was coming into the world (John 1: 6-9).

- And this is the judgment: the light has come into the world, and people loved the darkness rather than the light because their works were evil. For everyone who does wicked things hates the light and does not come to the light, lest his works should be exposed. But whoever does what is true comes to the light, so that it may be clearly seen that his works have been carried out in God (John 3:19-21).

- Again Jesus spoke to them, saying, "I am the light of the world. Whoever follows me will not walk in darkness, but will have the light of life." (John 8:12).

- So Jesus said to them, "The light is among you for a little while longer. Walk while you have the light, lest darkness overtake you. The one who walks in the darkness does not know where he is going. While you have the light, believe in the light, that you may become sons of light."

  When Jesus had said these things, he departed and hid himself from them (John 12:35-36).

- I am sending you to open their eyes, so that they may turn from darkness to light and from the power of Satan to God, that they may receive forgiveness of sins and a place among those who are sanctified by faith in me (Acts 26:17-18).

- For at one time you were darkness, but now you are light in the Lord. Walk as children of light (Ephesians 5:8).

- But you are a chosen race, a royal priesthood, a holy nation, a people for his own possession, that you may proclaim the excellencies of him who called you out of darkness into his marvelous light (1 Peter 2:9).

- This is the message we have heard from him and proclaim to you, that God is light, and in him is no darkness at all. If we say we have fellowship with him while we walk in darkness, we lie and do not practice the truth (1 John 1:5-6).

- But if we walk in the light, as he is in the light, we have fellowship with one another, and the blood of Jesus his Son cleanses us from all sin (1 John 1:7).

- Whoever says he is in the light and hates his brother is still in darkness. Whoever loves his brother abides in the light, and in him there is no cause for stumbling. But whoever hates his brother is in the darkness and walks in the darkness, and does not know where he is going, because the darkness has blinded his eyes (1 John 2:9-11).

- And the city has no need of sun or moon to shine on it, for the glory of God gives it light, and its lamp is the Lamb (Revelation 21:23).

Bibliography

Asimov, Isaac, ed., *The Human Brain*, New York: The New American Library, 1963.

Adler, Mortimer, *Great Books of the Western World.* Chicago: Encyclopedia Britannica Inc., 1993.

Allers, Rudolf, M.D., Ph.D., *What's Wrong with Freud?* Fort Collins, CO: Roman Catholic Books, 1960.

Bible, English Standard Version.

Biggs, Alton, Whitney Crispen Hagins, Chris Kapricka, et.al. *Biology, The Dynamics of Life*. Ohio: McGraw-Hill, 2004.

Boisen, Anton T., *Out of the Depths*. New York: Harper Brothers, 1960.

Boisen, Anton T., *The Exploration of the Inner World*. New York: Harper & Brothers, 1936.

Bonnano, George A. Ph.D., *Spirituality and Health Conference, Loss, Trauma, and Resilience: From Heterogeneity to Flexibility*. Chicago: Northwestern Medicine, July 22, 2015.

Bonnell, John S., *Psychology for Pastor and People*, New York: Harper and Brothers, 1948.

Bradberry, Travis and Jean Greaves, *Emotional Intelligence 2.0*. California: TalentSmart Publishing, 2009.

Campbell, Neil, Jane Reece, and Lawrence Mitchell, *Biology, Fifth ed*. California: Addison, Wesley, Longman Inc., 1987.

Cannon, Walter M.D., *The Wisdom of the Body*. New York: Norton and Co., 1932.

Carr, Harvey A., *Psychology, A Study of Mental Activity*. New York: Longmans, Green, and Co., 1926.

Chen, Y., Gibbs, M.E., et. al., *Astrocytic Adrenoceptors: A Major Drug Target in Neurological and Psychiatric Disorder?* United Arab Emirates: Bentham Science Publishers Ltd., 2004.

Cousins, Norman, *Head First, the Biology of Hope*. New York: E.P. Dutton, 1989.

Cummings, Des, Jr., PhD, Reed, Monica, MD. *Creation Health DISCOVERY*. Florida Hospital Publishing, Orlando, Florida, 2005.

Dashiell, John Frederick, *Fundamentals of Objective Psychology*. Cambridge: The Riverside Press, 1928.

Eckstein, Gustav, *The Body Has a Head*. New York: Harper and Row, 1970.

Encyclopedia Britannica. Chicago: Encyclopedia Britannica, Inc., 1993.

Epitome of the Pharmacopeia and National Formulary, ninth edition. Philadelphia, JB Lippincott Co., 1951.

Faculty.Washington.edu

Faddis, Margene O., R.N, M.A., *Textbook of Pharmacology*. Philadelphia: J.B. Lippincott Company, 1943.

Goleman, Daniel, *Emotional Intelligence*, United States: Bantam Books, 1995.

Hollingsworth, H.L., Ph.D., and A.T. Poffenberger, Ph.D., *Applied Psychology*, New York: D. Appleton and Company, 1925.

Howell, William, H., *A Textbook of Physiology for Medical Students and Physicians*. London: W.B. Saunders Co., 1916.

Hubel, David, H., *The Brain*. New York: Scientific American magazine, 1990.

Klein, Raymond, *Donald Olding Hebb*, Scholarpedia.org. Canada: Dalhousie University, 2011.

Kurzweil, Ray, *How to Create a Mind*. New York: Penguin Group, 2012.

Lickona, Thomas, *Character Matters*. New York: Touchstone Publishing, 2004.

Linnemann, Eta, *Historical Criticism of the Bible, Methodology or Ideology*, MI: Kregel Publications, 2001.

Luckman Joan, and Sorensen, *Medical-Surgical Nursing, A Psychophysiologic Approach*.

Philadelphia: W.B. Saunders Co.1980.

Marvelli, C.L., *Donald Hebb*, www.neuroswag.wordpress.com.

Neuroscience. Med.virginia.edu. University of Virginia: Rector and Board of Visitors, 2016.

Meldolesi, Jacopa and Volterra, Andrea, Nature review Neuroscience, 1 August 2005, internet, Nature.com, article called, *"Astrocytes, from Brain Glue to Communication Elements.*

Pancerz, Krzysztof and Elena Zaitseva, *Computational Intelligence, Medicine, and Body,*

Paolo Maria Rossini PM, et al. *Integrated technology for evaluation of brain function and neural plasticity.* physical medical rehabilitation clinic online, 2004.

Psychopharmacology. Washington DC: American Psychiatric Press, Inc., 1991.

Restak, Richard, M.D., *The Brain, The Last Frontier.* New York: Warner Books, 1979.

Schatzberg, Alan F., M.D., and Jonathan O. Cole, M.D., *Manual of Clinical*

The Compact Oxford English Dictionary, Second ed. New York: Oxford University Press, 1966.

The Revolution Continues." 2016 Macmillan Publishers Limited. PubMed doi:10.1038/nrn1722

Trojan, S, et al. *Plasticity of the Brain in Neuron ontogenesis.* Pubmed Online, 2004.

Trojan, S, et al *Theoretical aspects of neuroplasticity.* Pubmed Online, 2004.

Tweedie, Donald F., *Logotherapy and the Christian Faith.* Grand Rapids, MI.: Baker Book House, 1965.

Walter, Henrik, transl. by Cynthia Klohr, *Neurophysiology of Free Will.* Massachusetts: MIT Press, 2009.

Wright, John S., *A Guide to the Organic Drugs of the United States Pharmacopoeia, fifth edition.* Indianapolis, IN: Eli Lilly and company, 1926.

Zhuo, Lang, Biao Sun, et. at., *Live Astrocytes Visualized by Green Fluorescent Protein in Transgenic Mice.* (Science Direct.com. WI: UWI-Madison, 2002).

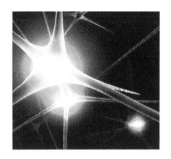

Endnotes

1. *The Compact Oxford English Dictionary,* 2nd ed. (Oxford University Press, 1999) 992.

2. Asimov, Isaac, *The Human Brain,* (New York: The New American Library, 1963) 117.

3. Ibid 319.

4. Hollingsworth, H.L., Ph.D., and A.T. Poffenberger, Ph.D., *Applied Psychology,* (New York: D. Appleton and Company, 1925) 25.

5. *The New Encyclopedia Britannica,* (Encyclopedia Britannica, 1994) 787.

6. Lickona, Thomas, *Character Matters,* (New York: Touchstone Publishing, 2004) 285.

7. Bradberry and Greaves, *Emotional Intelligence 2.0,* (California: TalentSmart Publishing, 2009) 296.

8. http://www.mysuburbanlife.com/2010/07/06/many-mourn-surgeon-at-funeral/zohsrmf/?page=2

9. Dashiell, John Frederick, *Fundamentals of Objective Psychology,* (Cambridge: The Riverside Press, 1928) 254.

10. *Encyclopedia Britannica* 835.

11. Bradberry and Greaves 62.

12. Goleman, Daniel, *Emotional Intelligence,* (United States: Bantam Books, 1995) 15.

13. Carr, Harvey A., *Psychology, A Study of Mental Activity,* (New York: Longmans, Green, and Co. 1926) 26.

14. Ibid. 184.

15. Adler, Mortimer, *Great Books of the Western World,* (Chicago: Encyclopedia Britannica Inc., 1993) 742.

16. Carr 312.

17. Ibid. 319.

18. Adler 712.

19. Carr 319.

20. Walter, Henrik, transl. by Cynthia Klohr, *Neurophysiology of Free Will,* (Massachusetts: MIT Press, 2009) 115.

21. Ibid.

22. Marvelli, C.L., Donald Hebb, www.neuroswag.wordpress.com.

23. Dashiell 254.

24. Cannon, Walter M.D., *The Wisdom of the Body,* (New York: Norton and Co., 1932) 229.

25. Restak, Richard, M.D., *The Brain, The Last Frontier,* (New York: Warner Books, 1979) 310.

26. Eckstein, Gustav, *The Body has a Head,* (New York: Harper and Row, 1970) 100.

27. Faculty.washington.edu online

28. Ibid.

29. Ibid.

30. Bonnano, George A. Ph.D., Spirituality and Health Conference, Loss, Trauma, and Resilience: From Heterogeneity to Flexibility. (Chicago: Northwestern Medicine, July 22, 2015).

31. Paolo Maria Rossini PM, et al. Integrated technology for evaluation of brain function and neural plasticity, (physical medical rehabilitation clinic online, 2004).

32. Faddis, Margene O., R.N, M.A., *Textbook of Pharmacology*, (Philadelphia: J.B. Lippincott Company, 1943) 23.

33. *A Guide to the Organic Drugs of the United States Pharmacopoeia, fifth edition*, (Indianapolis, IN: Eli Lilly and company, 1926) 1.

34. *Astrocytes: The Free Dictionary* by Farlex, http://medical-dictionary.thefreedictionary.com/astrocytes, accessed 2-26-2016.

35. Hubel, David, H., "The Brain." *New York: Scientific American Magazine*, 1990.

36. *The Compact Oxford English Dictionary, 2nd ed.*, (Oxford University Press, 1999) 1465.

37. Ibid. 82.

38. Howell, William, H., *A Textbook of Physiology for Medical Students and Physicians*, (London: W.B. Saunders Co., 1916) 183.

39. Meldolesi, Jacopa and Volterra, Andrea," Astrocytes, from Brain Glue to Communication (Nature.com. 1 August 2005) 628.

40. Zhuo, Lang, Biao Sun, et. at., Live Astrocytes Visualized by Green Fluorescent Protein in Transgenic Mice. (Science Direct.com. WI: UWI—Madison, 2002).

41. Campbell, Neil, Jane Reece, and Lawrence Mitchell, *Biology, 5th Ed.*, (California: Addison, Wesley, Longman Inc., 1987) 172.

42. Ibid. 180.

43. Adler 135.

44. Howell, William, H., *A Textbook of Physiology for Medical Students and Physicians*, (London: W.B. Saunders Co., 1916) 103.

45. Meldolesi and Volterra 628.

46. Campbell, et al. 204.

47. Ibid.

48. Allers, Rudolf, M.D., Ph.D., *What's Wrong with Freud?* (Fort Collins, CO: Roman Catholic Books 1960) 112.

49. Campbell, et al. 175.

50. Adler 423.

51. Adler 372.

52. *The Compact Oxford English Dictionary.*

53. Ibid.

54. Bonnell, John S., *Psychology for Pastor and People*, (New York: Harper and Brothers, 1948) 29.

55. Ibid. 16.

56. Linnemann, Eta, *Historical Criticism of the Bible, Methodology or Ideology*, (MI: Kregel Publications, 2001) 156.

57. Tweedie, Donald F., *Logotherapy and the Christian Faith,* (Grand Rapids, MI.: Baker Book House, 1965) 152.

58. www.goodreads.com

59. Adler, 54.

60. Ibid. vi

61. Ibid. 218

62. Ibid. 154.

63. Ibid. 295.

64. Tweedie, 101.

65. Ibid.

To dialogue with the author on this topic
and to learn about the nervous system,
please visit Colleen Lanigan online at:

www.neurohealthsystems.com

lanigan.colleen@yahoo.com

Made in the USA
Las Vegas, NV
24 April 2021

21945022R00068